Mamacita

Mamacita

Recipes Celebrating Life as a Mexican Immigrant in America

Andrea Pons

Foreword by **Hetty Lui McKinnon**

PRINCETON ARCHITECTURAL PRESS · NEW YORK

Published by
Princeton Architectural Press
70 West 36th Street
New York, NY 10018
www.papress.com

For Princeton Architectural Press
Editor: Holly La Due
Production editor: Sara Stemen
Design concept: Matt Ogle
Designers: Paul Wagner and Natalie Snodgrass
Indexer: Elizabeth Parson

For the self-published edition
Editor and indexer: Erin Motley
Assistance by Kristina Capulong and Kasama Space

Photography Credits
Marissa Alves: pages 27, 39, 66, 73, 77, 83, 87, 89, 101, 105,
    113, 121, 122, 132, 137, 147, 155, 166, 185, 188
Delaney Brown: pages 32, 84, 143, 171, 172, 182
Talia Green: pages 49, 80
Brian Oh: pages 2, 118, 129, 144, 169
AJ Ragasa: pages 21, 28, 31, 36, 43, 46, 50, 54, 57, 60, 65,
    70, 74, 92, 98, 102, 106, 110, 135, 150, 160, 164, 176, 181
Carina Skrobecki: pages 6, 24, 126
May Xiong: page 40

Props and styling by Andrea Pons except for pages 24, 40,
    49, 80, 101, and 126

Library of Congress Cataloging-in-Publication Data
Names: Pons, Andrea, 1994– author.
Title: Mamacita / Andrea Pons.
Description: New York : Princeton Architectural Press,
    [2022] | Includes index. | Summary: "A love letter to
    author Andrea Pons's native Mexico, weaving stories of
    her family's immigration to the United States with 75
    delicious recipes from three generations of women in her
    family"—Provided by publisher.
Identifiers: LCCN 2022001371 (print) | LCCN 2022001372
    (ebook) | ISBN 9781648961717 (hardcover) |
    ISBN 9781648961960 (ebook). Subjects: LCSH: Cooking,
    Mexican. | Pons, Andrea, 1994– | LCGFT: Cookbooks.
Classification: LCC TX716.M4 P65 2022 (print) | LCC TX716.
    M4 (ebook) | DDC 641.5972—dc23/eng/20220213. LC
    record available at https://lccn.loc.gov/2022001371.
    LC ebook record available at https://lccn.loc.
    gov/2022001372

FOR MY PARENTS, who have taught me that things don't happen to us, they happen for us. Thank you for all of your sacrifices, your love, and always making life feel adventurous.
I love you.

CONTENTS

FOREWORD

I am the third child of immigrants from Guangdong province in China. I grew up in the suburbs of Sydney, Australia, where our washed laundry dried on the line next to salted fish, pork, and duck being preserved for future meals. From a young age, I knew I was different from the other kids at school. This feeling of isolation, of being "the other," was a silent struggle which carried me through school, university, my early career, and followed me into motherhood. It is hard to accept who you are when the world is always telling you to be someone else.

There is a lot I have forgotten about my life but there are also moments that I remember with absolute clarity. These seemingly fleeting occurrences from my daily life as a Chinese girl growing up in Australia have stuck with me, and I still fight the shame that comes with these memories. I remember being banished to ESL (English as a Second Language) class in kindergarten, even though I spoke English fluently. I recall a childhood birthday party where a parent asked me what my real name was because it definitely could not have been *Hetty*, and the time a high school economics teacher demanded to know who helped me with my essay because there was no way I could have written it on my own. What is interesting is that, at the time, I did not feel anger towards the person belittling me, but I felt a deep humiliation for who I was and what I looked like. I ached to be accepted as Australian, without questions or caveats.

My experience is, sadly, not unique. Almost two decades later, on the other side of the Pacific, Andrea Pons, the author of this spectacular debut cookbook, was settling into a new life in White Center, Washington, near Seattle. As she sat in ESL class, Andrea felt singled out and ostracized. In the playground, she was harassed by classmates who wanted to see her green card, while others threatened to call ICE on her family. As an immigrant, Andrea's right to live in the United States was constantly questioned. Her "citizenship" was conditional, dependent upon her muting her "foreignness" to fit in. This is a prerequisite that immigrants, and their children, know well.

Immigrants are connected by the discomfort that comes from being an outsider. But in recent years, I have come to understand that there are also positives that come with living life on the peripheries, as we see with this book. In *Mamacita*, we read the story of a young Mexican woman who found salvation in the kitchen, emancipated from the fear that she would never be enough. Cooking the food and flavors of her childhood and her heritage provided Andrea with the narrative to embrace her "whole self." And her liberation feels like a precious gift to readers and home cooks. Andrea's soul shines brightly and with constancy on every page and in every recipe. Her voice sparkles with resilience, tenacity, courage, passion, and that indelible trait that we find in immigrants, hope. Food is sustenance, nourishment, and enjoyment, but for many, it is freedom.

The American dream is subjective. For many, it is rooted in the opportunity for prosperity, professional success, social mobility, and material riches. For Andrea, her American dream is simpler—to send her parents back home to Mexico to visit their families, with the knowledge that they would be able to re-enter the United States, safely. For every person who holds a copy of *Mamacita* in their hands, and cooks one of Andrea's delicious recipes, there is the special knowledge that we not only are contributing to Andrea's American dream, but we are building a community of kindness that will extend to immigrant communities all over the world. In *Mamacita*, we can all find a way to celebrate togetherness and unbreakable family bonds. I'm proud to be Team Pons, all the way.

—Hetty Lui McKinnon

Andrea's parents, Francisco Pons and Lorena Lopez

EMBRACING MY ROOTS:
An Immigrant's Story

My dad was sitting on the edge of his bed with the newspaper spread across his body. In my favorite pajamas with hair still wet from a shower, I roamed through a trove of objects in the drawer of my dad's nightstand. I picked up an old army watch that belonged to my grandfather. The subtle scent of vanilla surrounded the statue of La Virgen de Guadalupe, watching us with the slightest hint of a smile. I watched the flame dancing to the tune of the nightly gossip show *Ventaniando* on TV. My mom only lit a candle under the Virgin when she was deeply worried. When I kissed my parents on their cheeks before heading off to bed, my Papi looked down at me and casually asked, "What do you think about us moving to the United States for a few years?"

At nine years old, I spent all night imagining my life in the United States, dreaming of riding yellow school buses and eating peanut butter sandwiches for lunch just like they did in the movies. I fell asleep thinking about all of the stories I would be able to tell my friends when we returned.

Our home was known as the neighborhood petting zoo. I had two dogs and several street cats in addition to parrots, iguanas, frogs, turtles, and snakes. I didn't know what moving meant—we had never even moved between houses—but things began to disappear. Every day, after school, I came home to one fewer beloved pet. My favorite stuffed animal, a bunny in a dress gifted to me on my birthday, was passed down to my youngest cousin. It was becoming clear that this move was more than temporary.

I knew my parents were struggling with money even though no one mentioned it. Once, debt collectors came to our house and removed beautiful pieces of furniture from our home. I remember my nanny yelling at them to get a job that didn't ruin people's lives. Some mornings, my parents didn't get out of bed; I had to go to my neighbor's house so they could take me to school. Years later, I learned my dad's business was going poorly. He owned a manufacturing company that produced machines for leather tanneries. There was a recession in Mexico, and people owed him money for the machines and services. Often, my dad had terrible headaches caused by anxiety and depression.

On my dad's fortieth birthday, my Tio Christian arrived to take us to the airport. I knew our family was struggling. Secretly, I had stuffed an alcancia (piggy bank) with 50 pesos. That morning, I smashed it against my wall and placed the money I'd saved, less than two dollars, in my mom's hands. We would always be Team Pons. Silently, I said goodbye to everything I knew by heart, everything I'd known and loved. Adiós backyard bougainvillea tree. Adiós sparrow's nest, appearing like magic every spring just above our front door.

Adiós my little home and basketball hoop. Adiós Jassá middle school. Adiós corner store. Adiós cousins. Adiós León, mi casa.

On my very first flight, I held onto a photo of my best friends and cried.

We had close family friends who were already living in Washington State. They had moved five years earlier and encouraged my parents to do the same. In my dad's words, we moved because he wanted to see how my sister Vanessa and I would do. When my parents saw my sister and me adapting to a future with possibilities, they sold our home in Mexico.

When I look back on my childhood, it often feels like I am remembering someone else's life. Running barefoot on the grass of my grandmother Titita Tere's backyard. The cheap rose-scented lotion my mother slathered on me after a shower. Weekends when my Papi would drive my sister and me in the 1957 mustard-yellow Jeep that he fixed up himself. Hikes to the hills surrounding our hometown, searching for arrowheads and fossils buried in the soil. Critters we caught, small lizards and skinny snakes, and brought to our home. I'm even more thankful for these memories since I haven't been back.

As a kid, I lived my life balancing on a tightrope between being myself and the person who others expected me to be. In León, my sister and I went with shoes shined and nails clipped to a strict Catholic school, where the teachers would send us home if our hair wasn't gelled up. When my family moved to the States, my life still felt like a balancing act, but the platforms were much higher and the language had changed. Being a tomboy versus a polished, proper student was no longer my biggest concern. Instead, I was wavering between being Mexican and hiding behind a white-presenting self. We were living in a new country, but the threat of being sent back home still carried the same dread that came with being deemed dirty by an authority figure in front of your peers. It made me feel small and unfit for love. And I wondered, *Am I good enough to stay?*

ON MY FIRST DAY of school in the United States, I discovered I didn't fit in before I'd even walked into the classroom. In Mexico, you greeted your teacher with a kiss at the door before sitting down at your desk. When I gave my American teacher the same greeting, he tensed up and awkwardly ushered me inside. I remember feeling embarrassed, as if I had done something wrong.

My family wasn't familiar with the colder Northwest seasons. One day, my mom sent me to school in three layers of clothing. I walked into class wearing snow pants and a snow jacket, a suit made complete with snow gloves. I felt like Randy from *A Christmas Story*, except it was October, and there was no snow. Unfortunately, this coincided with a class field trip, so I spent the day roasting

inside a tailored sleeping bag while my classmates made fun of me. It was like showing up to school in the wrong pair of shoes. I did this, too. I remember the shame of feeling different and wanting so badly to fit in. However, what I wore gave me away and screamed that I wasn't from here.

I was desperate to learn English and feel like a normal kid. Instead of going to homeroom class to work on fun and creative projects, I got sent to ESL class. It made me feel like I wasn't good enough or smart enough to join my classmates. Since I was only one of four kids sent to ESL out of the entire public school, I felt singled out. So, I started skipping ESL and showing up to homeroom even if I had no clue what was going on. At home, I spent hours watching American television with subtitles to learn English as quickly as possible.

ONE MISCONCEPTION people communicated to me is that Mexican people only fit one profile. Because I don't have brown skin, my Mexican identity was constantly in question. Often, racial bias and microaggressions targeted something I couldn't hide, my accent. What hurt the most was discovering my own voice could betray me. Classmates harassed me, asking me to prove myself. "You don't look Mexican. Say something in Spanish," they'd say. "Show us your green card."

I didn't even know there was a wall separating these two countries until I was living in the States. People assumed I had moved here illegally, thinking I had crossed the border in the back of a truck or ran across the desert. For me, the border is a reminder that the government is trying to protect the United States from people like me. The wall specifically made me feel like I didn't belong here. When a racist classmate discovered I was Mexican, he came to school the next day wearing a T-shirt with a drawing of a wall and stick figures on one side. The shirt said, "Get back to your side."

To this day, I have never been to the border. Even now, I'm afraid if I get too close, I would be stopped and interrogated, separated from my family, and sent back to Mexico.

I grew up afraid to be myself: to be Mexican. This is a fear my parents didn't intend to pass on to me, but it was damaging nonetheless. My parents tried to protect my sister and me, encouraging us to say we were "Mexican-Italian," but I couldn't identify because it wasn't true. Still, I never felt like I could own up to the truth that I am Mexican-born because I was scared of being rejected and terrified of being deported. So, I lied to fit in.

When people asked about my legal status, I would lie and say I had a green card. At school, kids threatened to call ICE on my family. I felt terrified and helpless because one day, ICE did show up at the house of Mexican friends and took their dad away. I've always feared Team Pons could one day be separated.

A big misconception about immigrants is that we don't work hard, relying on the government to take care of us. This notion couldn't be further from the truth because the government does not help immigrants unless they have status. People assumed my parents worked physical jobs in cleaning and construction because they were uneducated. The fact is that both of my parents are college graduates. Since my dad's visa had expired, and the renewal process took so long, my parents worked those jobs to support our family.

When everyone else was applying for college, my immigration status presented me with a new set of obstacles. For me, higher-level education was immediately ruled out due to the cost; my immigration status made me ineligible for federal loans and student aid reserved for citizens and permanent residents. It was 2008, and my family was, once again, dealing with the financial struggles of a recession and the possibility of losing our home to the bank. My parents told me they were unable to afford the cost of college. It was up to me to make it happen. For years, I earned money as a babysitter, but it wasn't close to being enough. In 2011, I applied to a local community college with tuition costs I still couldn't afford.

In the summer of 2012, President Obama passed Deferred Action for Childhood Arrivals (DACA). I was seventeen years old. Finally, a path was created for children like me, bringing us one step closer to permanent status. Thanks to DACA, I was able to get a work permit, allowing me to work at an IHOP chain making $7.50 per hour as a host. I applied to any and all scholarships that did not require me to disclose my status. Out of eighty scholarships, I received five, which paid my tuition costs in full. With the money I earned from working, I moved out of my parents' home and rented a room in a house. I continued to work part-time through college to make ends meet.

At twenty-three years old, I thought I had made it. I had a lifelong partner, an apartment to call home, a career, and good friends. Sometimes, it takes something traumatic to wake you up to the fact that things still need to change. Three months after my twenty-fourth birthday, I found myself single, divorced, and living alone. For the first time, I discovered I was living my life for other people and not for myself.

That summer, I was sicker than I'd ever been, fighting illness after illness and stomachaches from constant stress. My body and self had diverged. I no longer wanted to feel disconnected, so I started cooking at home. The food I made offered a new identity, creating a path that led me back to myself as a Mexican immigrant. With no one to tell me what I could and couldn't cook, I started to make the dishes that I missed from my childhood. It was a chance to rediscover my heritage and an opportunity to heal. Cooking these dishes was an act of self-love for the part of myself whose country said I was never enough and could never fit in.

When I began writing this cookbook four years ago, I had an expired green card. I received an official letter from the government stating I had two years to apply for citizenship or an extension. My path to citizenship is both unique and common. The immigration system is a labyrinth, and while many of us find ourselves in the same maze, finding our way out is a personal puzzle that we are often left to figure out on our own.

Applying for citizenship as a Mexican immigrant requires a level of privilege greater than most have access to or can afford. I didn't make enough money, and my family didn't either. I had to ask our family friend Vicente, who then worked for Boeing, to be my sponsor, which was not a small request. Essentially, he signed a contract stating that he would be financially responsible for me if I lost my job or declared bankruptcy. If Vicente had been unable to aid me financially, then the government could have sued him. Thanks to Vicente, I was able to start the application process. He has since passed, but I will never forget Vicente's kindness and the generosity he extended to our family.

People who believe immigration is quick and uncomplicated haven't gone through the system. It's intimidating and confusing for everyone, especially those who have to go through it. It's almost impossible to start without being financially stable. Often, people assume we aren't paying taxes. Even if we don't have status, we still pay taxes. The process of obtaining status can take a very long time. It took me fifteen years. Navigating the system is never easy because immigration laws frequently change, adding higher costs to the increased complexity.

In June 2020, I was confronted by the reality of deportation, and I've never been more scared. In a panic, I called my immigration lawyer, a privilege not everyone has, and discovered I had to start the application process all over again. Ten years of previous immigration paperwork no longer applied to my case. When that happens, you have no choice but to start over. For the record, there are no refunds for the applications that no longer apply. Ten thousand dollars later, I found myself on a new path toward the same goal.

OPPOSITE
Original recipe book and card written by Andrea's grandmother Titita Tere; business card from Tere's bakery La Española; and photograph of Andrea's mother at a market

Andrea's childhood costume made by her mother

UPROOTING MY LIFE taught me that the only thing we can expect is everything we didn't plan to happen. Months after the initial call to my lawyer, I sat at the office of the United States Citizenship and Immigration Services (USCIS), waiting to see whether I had passed the test. After spending two hours answering a series of life-altering questions, I did it. I achieved my parents' dream, my dream—the American dream. With a certificate in one hand and a dollar-store American flag gripped in the other, I could finally call myself a citizen of the United States.

Today, in a pandemic, we are reckoning with the fact that racism is just as prevalent as it's ever been. Millions of immigrants are still dealing with the heartbreaking process of obtaining safety in a country they have called home for years, my parents and sister included. I want to dedicate this cookbook to all of you, to all of the immigrant families who packed up your lives and came to America for the chance to see your children grow up, accomplishing the things you could only dream about before leaving behind the world you once knew.

Mamacita, titled after my father's nickname for my mother, is my family's legacy. The recipes in this book were developed by women who are hardworking, brave, and always ready to assert themselves. One day, my grandmother Titita Tere rolled up her sleeves and decided to bake. She sold cakes out of her kitchen window for very cheap, the equivalent of $2.25 in today's dollars. Eventually, she began baking coffee cakes, birthday cakes, and custom wedding cakes. Her baked goods became so popular she opened a brick-and-mortar bakery in 1968, the same year my mom was born, and named it La Española.

When my grandfather died in a work accident, my Titita was left with six children to raise. The bakery became a family-run business. My oldest tias worked in the kitchen, baking and decorating cakes. My tios loaded up the vans before sunrise, delivering fresh loaves and baked goods across town just in time for desayuno. Titita Tere never remarried. She sent all of her children to college with the income she earned from La Española.

My mom was only eleven years old when her father passed away, and her youngest sibling Lalo was just a toddler. At the time, my grandma was always busy with the bakery as a single mother. My mom, the second youngest, would sometimes work the register and write down customers' orders. Surrounded by strong women and raised by her two older sisters, Leni in particular, my mom grew up to be an independent woman of many trades.

Although my mom has a bachelor's degree in textile design, she couldn't find a job due to her status once we moved to the United States. Rather than feeling defeated or giving up, she immediately found a position as a house cleaner. No job was ever beneath my mom; she always found a way to provide and

passed down her ability to be resourceful to my sister and me.

I always loved watching my mom sewing in the TV room, listening to the steady hum of her machine and seeing her joy as she focused on her home business. She designed and constructed dresses for every occasion: First Communions, Halloween, and weddings. She made clothing for my sister and me throughout our lives. Back in Mexico, she had her dream job, designing for a children's clothing company. My mom quit her job to marry my dad and raise two daughters, but she never lost the passion she continues to bring to every project she tackles.

My mom always encourages us to follow our interests regardless of the status quo. When a karate school opened up and I wanted to take a class, even though I was already a cheerleader, my mom was the first to enroll my sister and me. She has always been more forward-thinking than most of her friends, who considered karate to be a gendered sport for boys. I admire the way she empowers us to try new things and direct our own lives.

I hate to admit that I was afraid to show up as a Mexican immigrant. I spent years living in shame, feeling like I could never be enough. I feared people would call me an impostor and treat me as such. But being an immigrant and reclaiming my heritage isn't something I want to hide or make smaller. I'm proud of where I came from, how far I've traveled, and the experiences I've gathered along the way. Hardship, obstacles, and losses, too, have given me the courage and openness to appreciate even the smallest wins.

I know it sounds dramatic, but cooking saved my life. Making these dishes helped me crawl out of a dark place of hiding and provided a space where I could finally show up as my whole self. By immortalizing the recipes I grew up eating as a kid in Mexico, I reconnected with the part of myself I never meant to forget. As a Mexican immigrant, I want to voice my story by sharing my food with you.

In Mexico, time revolved around cooking and eating together as a family.

We even have a word for the extended time you spend with company around the dinner table over dessert and coffee. Sobremesa. It was a bigger deal on the weekends at my grandparents' home when the entire family would gather for dinner. Tita Maru's dinner table was big enough to seat her six children and their spouses. I would rush to kiss all of my tios' and tias' cheeks, trying my best not to miss a single cheek before taking my seat. If I missed greeting even one family member, it would be weeks before I stopped hearing about it. Looking back on all of the sobremesas we didn't share at Tita Maru's table, I'm glad I rarely missed a kiss.

My mother, like my grandmother, has yet to use a measuring spoon. Instead, she is guided by the palms of her hands, knowing by heart how much to add. I have written these recipes down, added measurements, and simplified the process so you can make my family's recipes on your own or invite the people you love to share a meal together.

There is no greater pleasure than serving food to the people you love and seeing the delight on their faces when they taste something made just for them. When you make these recipes, I hope you feel more connected to the immigrant communities around you. I want us to keep striving to show up, help other immigrants to speak up, and listen to each other's stories. Most of all, I hope my story reminds you to trust yourself. Wherever you are now, who you are meant to be is entirely up to you.

Salsas

Salsa Verde

Green Salsa / MAKES ABOUT 3 CUPS

Growing up, we had various types of salsas in the fridge at all times. But there were two that never ran out: salsa verde and salsa roja. My mama would make a fresh batch every weekend for the week ahead. This salsa verde is incredibly versatile and can be used in many dishes; my favorite ones are chilaquiles verdes and pozole verde. You can additionally top a quesadilla with this salsa, mix it into your guacamole for a spicy dip, or simply eat it with tortilla chips. The options are limitless.

9 ounces tomatillos
   (about 6), divided
1 tablespoon avocado oil
½ cup chopped white onion
2 fresh jalapeño peppers,
   seeded
1 canned jalapeño pepper
1 tablespoon fresh lime juice
½ cup chopped cilantro leaves
1 teaspoon sea salt

Peel off the tomatillos' paper husks and rinse under cold running water.

In a large saucepan, combine half of the tomatillos and enough water to cover them and bring to a boil over high heat. Reduce the heat to medium-high and cook for 3 minutes to soften the tomatillos. Remove the tomatillos with a slotted spoon and reserve ¼ cup of the cooking liquid.

Meanwhile, heat the oil over high heat. Sear the remaining tomatillos, flipping once, until brown, 1 to 2 minutes on each side. Remove from the heat.

In a blender, add all of the tomatillos and the reserved ¼ cup of liquid. Blend until smooth.

To the blender, add the chopped white onion, all of the jalapeños, the lime juice, cilantro, and salt. Blend until combined. Be careful not to liquify the salsa; it should be smooth with some texture. Taste and adjust the salt or lime juice as needed.

Transfer the salsa to a sealed container and refrigerate.

Salsa Roja

Red Salsa / MAKES ABOUT 3 CUPS

One of my favorite possessions as a kid was an early 2000s model folding pocket alarm clock that my papa brought back from one of his travels. Each morning before school, a gentle beeping sound would awake me to the smell of fresh scrambled eggs, warm tortillas, and a batch of salsa roja. This salsa was my favorite growing up and always had a place at our table, especially during breakfast. We ate all of our meals on that table regardless of having a much bigger dining room table, which was only used when my mama had her friends over. To this day, I still eat my scrambled eggs topped with salsa roja. This salsa is spicy, tangy, and a bit sweet, making it the perfect pairing for just about anything. Eggs? Tamales? Tortas? You name it. If you like your salsa a bit on the chunkier side, opt out of straining it to keep the texture.

Olive oil
2 medium tomatoes, halved
6 dried guajillo peppers,
    stems and seeds removed
1 dried pasilla pepper
    (or ancho pepper)
1 garlic clove
1 teaspoon sea salt

Preheat the oven to 450°F. Line a sheet pan with aluminum foil and drizzle with olive oil.

Arrange the tomatoes, skin-side down, on the sheet pan. Roast in the oven for 30 minutes.

Meanwhile, in a large saucepan, bring 3 cups of water to a boil over high heat. Add the dried peppers and cook until softened, about 3 minutes. Remove from the heat and set aside. Reserve 1 cup of the cooking liquid.

In a blender, add the roasted tomatoes, softened chiles, garlic, salt, and the reserved 1 cup of liquid. Blend until smooth.

Transfer the salsa to a sealed container and refrigerate.

If you want a smooth salsa without any pulp, strain the salsa to remove the pulp before transferring to a sealed container and refrigerating.

Enjoy with chips, on tacos, or in chilaquiles, huevos rancheros, or your favorite Mexican dish!

Pico de Gallo

Mexican Salsa / MAKES ABOUT 3 CUPS

The name of this salsa was inspired by the resemblance it has to the feathers of a rooster; the name "Pico de Gallo" translates to "rooster beak." In Mexico, we often also call this salsa "salsa fresca" or "salsa cruda" meaning fresh or raw, due to the fact that there is little to no cooking involved when making it. Pico de gallo is the most consumed salsa in the United States, but it often comes in plastic, containing faded-pink tomatoes that once were red, wilted cilantro, and most of the time zero flavor. There is really no excuse to buy this salsa when it is so easy to make! And it makes a great dish to dip your chips in at any party. If you want to mix things up, try adding some avocado, pineapple, or mango—I promise you won't regret it. And the next time you're eating a carnitas taco, make sure you don't skip the "pico."

3 medium Roma tomatoes, cored and diced
½ medium white onion, diced
1 jalapeño pepper, seeds removed, finely diced
1 tablespoon chopped cilantro leaves
1 large lime, juiced
Sea salt

In a medium bowl, combine the tomatoes, onion, jalapeño, and cilantro.

Add the fresh lime juice, mix with a spoon, and season with salt. Transfer the salsa to a sealed container and chill in the fridge.

Serve with tortilla chips.

Guacamole

MAKES ABOUT 3 CUPS

We all have experienced the "Yes, I know guac costs extra" moment in restaurants. And while guacamole has been a trend for the last couple of decades, this salsa dates back a millennium to when the Aztecs invented it. The origin of the word avocado is the Aztec word "ahu-catl." When the Spanish adopted the word, it became what is now "aguacate." And the word guacamole comes from the Aztec origin "ahuacamolli," which is a combination of the words for avocado and sauce, resulting in what we now know as guacamole. Guacamole can be considered one of the most ancient health-rich foods. Although the Aztecs were not aware of the nutritional facts of avocado, such as it being a source of healthy fats, fiber, and vitamins, they knew the effects the food had on their bodies and often considered avocados an aphrodisiac. In Mexico, most dishes are not complete without avocado slices or guacamole on the side. This delicious salsa is good enough to eat on its own, however, one of my favorite ways of eating it is by pairing it with meat. Try the Bistec con Guacamole on page 128.

4 ripe avocados
1 medium Roma tomato, cored and chopped
1 jalapeño pepper, seeds removed, finely diced
½ medium white onion, diced
¼ cup finely chopped cilantro leaves
1 teaspoon olive oil, plus more to taste
1 teaspoon sea salt, plus more to taste
1 to 2 large limes, juiced

In a medium bowl, mash the avocados with a fork. I like my guacamole a little chunky but mash to your desired texture. Add the tomato, jalapeño, onion, cilantro, olive oil, salt, and the juice of 1 lime. Gently mix with a spoon. Taste and adjust the olive oil, salt, lime juice as needed.

Serve with tortilla chips.

Verduras en Escabeche

Spicy Pickled Vegetables / MAKES ABOUT 3 CUPS

Every culture has its own version of pickled vegetables. In Korea, for example, they have kimchi, and in Mexico, Verduras en Escabeche is ours. A plate would feel incomplete without the presence of a pickled vegetable. I have been eating these delicious pickled spicy vegetables for as long as I can remember. When I was very little, the carrots were my favorite, and as I grew older, I couldn't eat a torta without pickled jalapeño. The beauty of these pickles is that you can really pickle whatever you want. Try adding baby corn, radishes, garlic, red onion—the possibilities are limitless.

1½ teaspoons olive oil
½ medium white onion, thinly sliced
4 garlic cloves
5 jalapeño peppers, halved lengthwise
2 rainbow carrots, peeled and cut into ¼-inch coins
1 red bell pepper, thinly sliced
1⅔ cups white vinegar, divided
¾ cup chopped cauliflower florets
Sea salt
2 tablespoons granulated sugar

In a large skillet, heat the oil over medium heat. Once the oil is shimmering, add the onion and garlic. Fry until the garlic turns golden brown. Add the jalapeños, carrots, and bell pepper. Continue to cook, stirring occasionally, until the vegetables soften, about 10 minutes. Add ⅔ cup of the white vinegar and bring to a boil over medium-high heat. Add the cauliflower and return to a boil. Season with salt and boil for 5 minutes. Remove from the heat.

In a medium saucepan, bring 1 cup of water, the remaining 1 cup of white vinegar, and the sugar to a boil over medium-high heat. Continue boiling for 1 minute then remove from the heat and let cool slightly. Taste and season with salt as needed.

Transfer the vegetables to a jar and top with the pickling liquid. Allow the pickles to cool completely before sealing with a lid. Chill in the fridge for at least 2 hours (or overnight).

Serve chilled. These will stay fresh for up to 2 weeks.

Ensaladas y Verduras

Ensalada de Calabacitas

Zucchini Salad / SERVES 4 TO 6

This is a super-simple salad, made to highlight the richness this end-of-summer vegetable has to offer. The key to this salad is to select zucchini that are ripe and young. Though best when zucchini are in season locally where you live, this salad can be eaten year-round. And although I grew up eating it sautéed, if you're making it at the height of zucchini season, you can create ribbons out of the vegetable and eat the salad raw.

4 tablespoons olive oil, divided
6 medium zucchinis, sliced into ½-inch wheels
Sea salt and ground black pepper
2 tablespoons white vinegar
⅛ teaspoon ground white pepper
¼ white onion, finely sliced
¼ cup crumbled Cotija cheese (or feta cheese)
¼ cup chopped cilantro leaves

In a large skillet, heat 1 tablespoon of the oil over medium heat. Add the sliced zucchini and sauté until tender but not too soft. Season with salt and black pepper. Set the zucchinis aside in a salad bowl.

In a small bowl, whisk together the remaining 3 tablespoons of oil, the vinegar, and white pepper. Season with salt.

To the salad bowl, add the onion and dressing and mix well.

Serve topped with crumbled Cotija and chopped cilantro.

Tortitas de Papa

Potato Pancakes / SERVES 4 TO 6

Potatoes are widely used in Mexican cuisine. You can see the evidence of this in potato-filled masa dishes, such as molotes; tacos dorados de papa; and Chiles Rellenos (page 42) filled with cheese and mashed or baked potatoes. They are also added to a variety of meat dishes such as Pollo en Adobo (page 127). In Mexico, Tortitas de Papa are a late-night favorite and can be found at street carts and market stands where people gather around to eat them fresh off the comal. They are delicious bathed in salsa with crema, and topped with queso Cotija. They can be eaten on their own as a snack or accompany a meal as a side dish.

6 medium baking potatoes, peeled and halved

2 large eggs

2 cups crumbled añejo cheese (or Cotija cheese)

Sea salt

All-purpose flour, for dusting

¼ cup avocado oil, plus more as needed for frying

In a large soup pot, combine the potatoes and 5 cups of water and bring to a boil over high heat. Reduce the heat to medium and cook until you can easily insert a butter knife through the potatoes, about 30 minutes. Transfer the potatoes to a large bowl and mash with a fork or potato masher until smooth. Add the eggs and añejo cheese, season with salt, and mix with your hands or a wooden spoon.

With lightly floured hands, form the potato mixture into 2-inch balls. Press down on the balls with your palm to create pancakes that are about 4 inches wide and ½ inch thick.

In a large, deep skillet, heat ¼ cup of avocado oil until it's hot but not smoking. Working in batches, fry the potato pancakes, flipping once, until golden-brown, 1 to 2 minutes on each side. You can add more avocado oil as needed to the skillet. Place the pancakes on a baking rack lined with paper towels to absorb any excess oil.

Serve hot.

Papaya con Hierbabuena

Papaya with Mint / SERVES 4 TO 6

During the summers, all the tias and all the cousins on my mama's side of the family would travel to Puerto Vallarta for a getaway. It was one of my favorite family vacations, and I looked forward to it like I looked forward to Christmas. Every morning, I would wake up to the sound of the bedroom ceiling fan in the villa, and the chatter of the mamas in the kitchen preparing breakfast for all the kids before a day at the beach. Papaya con Hierbabuena was a staple during these mornings. In Mexico, breakfast is a highly celebrated meal and fruit is an important part of completing it. Although I grew up eating fruit every morning, Papaya con Hierbabuena was reserved for the playa. Whenever I can get my hands on a good papaya, I recreate this fruit salad and it takes me right back to those days where my only worry was to avoid sunburn.

4 cups peeled, seeded, and
   cubed papaya, preferably
   Red Maradol
1 lime, juiced
1 bunch mint, chopped
⅔ cup granulated sugar

In a medium bowl, combine the papaya and lime juice. Fold in the mint. Add the sugar and stir again. Chill in the fridge for 5 to 10 minutes.
   Serve chilled.

Ensalada de Frutas

Fruit Salad / SERVES 4 TO 6

Most families in the United States have a staple fruit salad that either their mom, auntie, or grandma bring for the holidays. This is my familia's version of that fruit salad, but it's never reserved for a special occasion. In fact, making this salad is the occasion itself. This fruit salad celebrates tropical fruits—the combination of papaya, pineapple, and grapes is sure to make your day sunnier. Be sure to use only the freshest ingredients, and pick a pineapple that is on the riper side to avoid too much acidity in the salad.

1 cup granulated sugar

½ cup dry red wine

1 medium orange

1½ cups green seedless grapes

1 small cantaloupe, seeded and cubed

½ medium papaya, peeled, seeded, and cubed, preferably Red Maradol

1 cup peeled and cubed pineapple

In a saucepan, combine the sugar and ½ cup of water and bring to a boil over medium-high heat. Continue boiling until the sugar has dissolved, then turn off the heat, add the red wine, and set aside to cool.

With a sharp knife, remove the orange peel and pith. Slice and cube the orange and place in a large bowl. Add the grapes, cantaloupe, papaya, and pineapple and toss to combine. Chill in the fridge until ready to serve. Then bathe the fruit in the cooled wine sauce.

Serve chilled.

Chiles Rellenos

Stuffed Peppers / SERVES 6 TO 8

Peppers are some of the most widely used ingredients in Mexican dishes. We love to dry them, roast them, fry them, stuff them, and cover them in delicious sauces. We also like to slice them into strips and cook them into stews like Carne de Puerco con Rajas en Salsa de Tomate (page 134). But my personal favorite way to eat peppers is to roast them and stuff them, which is why chiles rellenos have been a favorite of mine throughout the years. Poblano peppers are the most commonly used peppers for stuffing in Mexico due to their size and sturdiness. Poblanos in the United States are a lot milder in flavor than in Mexico, where you can count on getting a spicy one. So, if you're looking for spicy, I recommend shopping for poblano peppers imported from Mexico or sourcing them from a local farm in your area during the summer months when they are in season. In addition, you can roast a large jalapeño and blend it into the sauce to make it spicy.

Stuffing fresh poblano peppers is a laborious task—you must roast them and peel them before you can stuff them. But the effort is well worth the reward. In this recipe I walk you through the process my mama used and the one most Mexicans use. This method can be applied to any pepper, and if you really feel like enchilarte (setting your mouth on fire), you can try this recipe with manzano chiles. But this is a chile that is sure to knock your socks off your feet, so be careful. Chiles rellenos are incredibly versatile; you can stuff them with melty cheese like I do in this recipe, add baked potatoes for a more filling meal, stuff them with refried beans, chicken, or even mushrooms. The choices are limitless.

FOR THE SAUCE
3 tablespoons olive oil
½ large white onion, sliced
4 garlic cloves, crushed
3 cups tomato sauce
1 tablespoon chicken
    bouillon powder

FOR THE CHILES RELLENOS
10 poblano peppers
7 large eggs, whites and
    yolks separated
Sea salt and ground
    black pepper
6 cups shredded
    mozzarella cheese
1 cup avocado oil
3 cups all-purpose flour

RECIPE CONTINUES →

Make the Sauce

In a medium saucepan, heat the olive oil over medium heat. Add the onion and sauté until it begins to soften. Add the garlic and cook for another 3 minutes.

Add the tomato sauce and chicken bouillon powder and bring to a boil. Reduce the heat to low and simmer until the sauce reduces, 5 to 7 minutes. Keep warm until ready to use.

Make the Chiles Rellenos

To torear (roast) the poblano peppers, place them directly over the flame of a gas stove or a grill. Turn occasionally until the skin begins to char and wrinkle on all sides. (Similarly, you can roast the poblano peppers in a 400°F oven for about 10 minutes, flipping the peppers halfway through.)

Chiles Rellenos / Stuffed Peppers

Place the peppers in an sealed container or a tightly knotted plastic bag to steam, allowing the peppers to soften as they cool.

When the peppers are cool enough to handle, gently remove the outer skin with your hands or a paper towel. Using your finger or a knife, make a small incision in each pepper. Be careful not to slice the peppers in half; you only need an opening big enough to stuff with cheese. Under cold running water, use your fingers to remove the seeds. Pat the peppers dry and set aside.

In a stand mixer, whisk the egg whites until stiff peaks begin to form. Continue to whisk the egg whites, adding one yolk at a time, and whisk until all the yolks are added and the mixture is fully combined. Generously season with salt and pepper.

Stuff each pepper with a generous amount of the mozzarella cheese. Bring the open edges of the peppers together, folding one edge over the other, and use a toothpick to keep the peppers closed—don't forget to remove them later.

In a large, deep pan, heat the avocado oil over medium heat.

Meanwhile, add the flour to a shallow bowl or plate. Gently roll the peppers in flour until covered. Dip each pepper in the egg mixture and carefully place into the avocado oil. Fry the chiles rellenos, flipping once, until golden brown, 2 to 3 minutes on each side. Place the chiles rellenos on a baking rack lined with paper towels to absorb any excess oil.

Serve with the sauce and enjoy.

TIP: My family traditionally eats this meal with a side of Arroz Rojo (page 86), beans, and warm tortillas.

Chiles en Nogada

Stuffed Peppers in Walnut Sauce / SERVES 4 TO 6

The state of Guanajuato in which I grew up, is known for *legends*, stories that have been passed down for generations. And chiles en nogada come with their own legend. The story often told about this dish is that it was first made by nuns in Puebla for the first president of Mexico, Agustin de Iturbide. And that its colors of red (pomegranate seeds), white (walnut sauce), and green (poblano pepper) were purposely chosen to represent the Mexican flag. However, the Mexican flag back then was red and blue. The dish's coloring can be better attributed to the fact that the main ingredients are in season in September—when, coincidentally, Mexican Independence Day takes place—and therefore it is most often made to celebrate the holiday. All households in Mexico have their own traditional version of this dish. Originally the recipe had pork, pineapple, and other dried fruits as filling, however, my family adapted this recipe to have plantains, apples, raisins, and pork instead. No matter how your family chooses to adapt the recipe, what is important is that the pepper, the sauce, and the pomegranate seeds are always present for it to truly be chiles en nogada.

FOR THE PEPPERS
6 large poblano peppers

FOR THE FILLING
1 plantain (not fully ripened, yellow with hints of green), ends trimmed and halved lengthwise (do not peel)
2 Roma tomatoes, quartered
4 tablespoons olive oil, divided
1 pound ground pork
½ teaspoon garlic powder
Sea salt and ground black pepper
1 teaspoon crushed Mexican dried oregano

½ teaspoon dried thyme
½ teaspoon dried marjoram
¼ teaspoon ground cinnamon
⅛ teaspoon ground cloves
1 small Fuji apple, diced
1 small white onion, diced
2 garlic cloves, minced
⅓ cup raisins

FOR THE SAUCE
1 cup walnuts
1 cup whole milk
4 ounces goat cheese
½ cup Mexican crema or sour cream
⅛ teaspoon ground cinnamon

1 tablespoon granulated sugar, plus more to taste (optional)
Sea salt

FOR SERVING
½ cup pomegranate seeds
½ cup chopped parsley leaves

RECIPE CONTINUES ⟶

Chiles en Nogada / Stuffed Peppers in Walnut Sauce

Make the Peppers

To torear (roast) the poblano peppers, place them directly over the flame of a gas stove or a grill. Turn occasionally until the skin begins to char and wrinkle on all sides. (Similarly, you can roast the poblano peppers in a 400°F oven for about 10 minutes, flipping the peppers halfway through.)

Place the peppers in an airtight container or a tightly knotted plastic bag to steam, allowing the peppers to soften as they cool.

When the peppers are cool enough to handle, gently remove the outer skin with your hands or a paper towel. Using your finger or a knife, make a small incision in each pepper. Be careful not to slice the peppers in half; you only need a cut big enough to stuff them. Under cold running water, use your fingers to remove the seeds. Pat the peppers dry and set aside.

Make the Filling

In a medium saucepan, bring 5 cups of water to a boil over high heat. Add the plantains, reduce the heat to medium, and cook for 15 minutes. Remove the plantains from the water and place on a baking rack to cool.

Meanwhile, in a blender, blend the tomatoes until smooth. Using a strainer, strain the tomatoes, and discard any large chunks. Set aside.

In a medium saucepan, heat 2 tablespoons of the oil over medium heat. Add the ground pork and garlic powder, season with salt and pepper, and cook for 10 minutes until the pork has browned. Add the herbs, spices, apple, onion, garlic, raisins, and the blended tomatoes and bring to a boil over medium-high heat, stirring occasionally. Reduce the heat to medium-low, and cook, partially covered so the steam can escape, for about 10 minutes.

Meanwhile, peel and finely dice the plantains. In a skillet, heat the remaining 2 tablespoons of the oil over medium heat. Fry the plantains in batches until crisp and golden.

Using a slotted spoon, add the fried plantains to the pork mixture and stir to combine. Continue cooking over medium-low heat until most of the liquid is absorbed, about 5 minutes. Remove from the heat and let cool.

Preheat the oven to 200°F.

Stuff each pepper with a generous amount of the pork mixture. Bring the open edges of the peppers together, folding one edge over the other, and use a toothpick to keep the peppers closed—don't forget to remove them later. Transfer the peppers to a baking dish, and place in the oven to keep warm while making the sauce.

Make the Sauce

In a blender, combine the walnuts, milk, goat cheese, sour cream, cinnamon, and sugar, if using. Season with salt and blend until smooth. The sauce should be sweet and tangy. Adjust the salt and sugar as needed.

To serve, ladle the sauce over each pepper and sprinkle with pomegranate seeds and parsley.

Elote Mexicano

Mexican Street Corn / SERVES 4 TO 6

After sixteen years of not traveling back home to Mexico due to the fear of being unable to return to my life in the United States as an immigrant, one of the first things I did as a citizen when I visited my family was to go out and get elote, also widely known as esquites, with my cousins. The tradition of eating this dish for merienda, or what we would call a "late-night snack" in the United States, has not changed since I left Mexico. It's hard to really explain what elote is: A soup? A salad? A dip? It's neither and all. And can either be served on the cob or in a cup or bowl. But what I do know is that esquites or elote are a favorite snack year-round, but especially in the fall when corn is plentiful, ripe, and fresh.

Sitting in my Titita Tere's patio with my primos, I ate esquites with one hand gripping the Styrofoam container, while adding ground chile piquin (chili powder), lime juice, Cotija cheese, and—if you're my cousin Carolina—Doritos, with the other before eating it all with a spoon. In Mexico, this is usually a to-go food, not something you would cook at home. However, since moving to the United States, it's something I often crave, and it's easy enough to make on any night (or day). Elote Mexicano is something you can enjoy hot, warm, or cold. So you could make a big batch for friends, or make enough for yourself to snack on during the week.

6 medium ears corn, shucked
1 tablespoon unsalted butter, melted
¼ cup mayonnaise
¼ cup Mexican crema or sour cream
1 tablespoon fresh lime juice, plus lime wedges, for serving
½ cup crumbled Cotija cheese
3 tablespoons chopped cilantro leaves
½ teaspoon chili powder
Sea salt

Preheat an outdoor grill to medium-high 375°F (or heat a grill pan over medium-high heat).

Brush each ear of corn with the melted butter.

Grill the corn, turning as it begins to brown. I prefer grilled corn on the browner side but not burnt.

Meanwhile, in a medium bowl, combine the mayonnaise, sour cream, and lime juice. Mix well.

Coat the grilled corn with the sauce and sprinkle with the Cotija cheese and cilantro. Season with chili powder and salt.

Serve with the lime wedges.

Frijoles Refritos

Refried Beans / SERVES 4 TO 6

Refried beans are a staple of Mexican cuisine and served as a side with almost any meal from breakfast to dinner. Traditionally, frijoles refritos are made with lard instead of vegetable oil. In my version, I use avocado oil which is a high-smoke point oil that is great for frying and allows the dish to be a vegetarian option. What I love about this recipe is that you could stop after step five and serve the beans in their liquid as frijoles aguados, which is another traditional way of eating beans in Mexico. Simply serve the beans in small bowls with some of their liquid, like soupy beans, and top with queso fresco. If you want the beans to be refried continue with the recipe. You can use any type of bean for this recipe, but I prefer black because of their flavor.

2 cups dried black beans
1 garlic clove
1 epazote sprig or
    1 tablespoon chopped
    fresh oregano
½ teaspoon sea salt, plus
    more as needed
¼ cup avocado oil
½ white onion, minced

TOPPINGS
Queso fresco

Rinse the beans with cold water to remove any dirt or debris.

Place the beans in a tall, medium clay pot and cover with about 1½ cups of water. If you don't have a clay pot, a medium heavy-bottomed pot will do, as long as there is enough room for the beans to expand as they hydrate.

Add the garlic and the epazote sprig or oregano to the beans and bring to a boil. Boil for 1 minute. Lower the heat, cover the pot, and gently simmer the beans for 30 minutes, stirring occasionally to make sure all the beans cook evenly. Add water as needed to maintain 3 inches or so of water above the beans. Cover and continue simmering for another 15 minutes. Take out one bean and taste for doneness. The beans will most likely not be completely tender yet. Cover and continue simmering, gently stirring occasionally and adding more water as needed, until the beans are soft, but their skins are not cracked. Check the beans every 5 to 10 minutes; if their skins crack, you've cooked them for too long.

RECIPE CONTINUES ⟶

Frijoles Refritos / Refried Beans

When satisfied with the texture, season with ½ teaspoon of salt. Discard the garlic clove and reserve 1 cup of the cooking liquid and drain the rest.

In a medium bowl, use a fork to mash the beans into a paste, making sure there are no beans left whole. Gradually add some of the reserved bean liquid as you go to help with the process. I like my refried beans with texture, however, if you prefer a smooth consistency, you can add the beans and liquid to a blender and blend until silky.

In a medium skillet, heat the oil over medium heat. Add the onion and cook until fragrant and translucent. Add the mashed beans and gently stir to incorporate the onion. Taste and season with salt as needed. Drizzle with more of the reserved bean liquid as needed to achieve the desired consistency. The texture should be a thick, creamy paste.

Serve topped with crumbled queso fresco, alongside your favorite dishes, or eat as a dip.

Ensalada de Betabeles

Beet Salad / SERVES 4 TO 6

Beets have always been one of my favorite root vegetables. When I was a kid, my mama once told me that they act as natural make-up, and that if I ate enough of them my cheeks would turn rosy. I believed her then and somehow still believe this is true. This salad is simple and delicious and complements any meat dish or can be mixed in a bed of greens with cooked brown rice or quinoa for a hearty lunch.

5 medium beets, peeled
½ white onion, thinly sliced
3 tablespoons olive oil
2 tablespoons white vinegar
¼ teaspoon sea salt, plus
    more to taste
¼ teaspoon ground black
    pepper

In a large saucepan, combine the beets and 5 cups of water and bring to a boil over high heat. Reduce the heat to medium and cook until you can easily insert a butter knife through the beets, 45 to 60 minutes. Remove the beets from the saucepan and cool them under cold running water. Set aside to cool.

When the beets are cool enough to handle, slice them into thin rounds, about ⅛- to ¼-inch thick. Set aside in a salad bowl with the onion.

In a lidded jar, combine the olive oil, vinegar, salt, and pepper, and shake to combine.

Bathe the beets and onions in the dressing. Season with salt.

Serve at room temperature or chilled.

Ensalada de Chayotes

Chayote Squash Salad / SERVES 4 TO 6

A vegetable? A fruit? Chayotes, also known as mirliton squash, are often called vegetable pears due to their shape. Chayote grows across Mexico and is enjoyed in many ways, but my favorite is in salad. I love this recipe because it gives the chayotes a soft texture and the salad pairs well with meat dishes. If you are short on time and want a quick snack, you can eat chayotes raw by julienning them, squeezing half a lime, adding a bit of olive oil, and tying everything together with Tajín (Mexican spicy-sour seasoning salt).

4 medium chayotes
1 tablespoon finely chopped
    white onion
2 tablespoons olive oil
1 tablespoon white
    wine vinegar
Sea salt and ground
    black pepper
Finely chopped cilantro
    leaves

Rinse the chayotes with cold water.

In a medium soup pot, combine the whole chayotes and enough water to completely submerge them. Bring to a boil for 1 minute, then cook over medium-high heat, until you can easily insert a butter knife through the chayotes, 15 to 20 minutes.

Using a ladle, remove the chayotes from the water and place on paper towels to dry. When the chayotes are still warm but cool enough to handle, peel them. Cut each chayote in half lengthwise, then scoop out the seed from the middle. Place cut-side down on a cutting board and slice the chayote into ¼-inch slices as you would an apple. Place in a serving bowl.

In a small bowl, mix the onion, oil, and vinegar. Season with salt and pepper. Bathe the chayotes in the vinaigrette, top with cilantro, and serve.

Tunas con Yogur

Prickly Pear with Yogurt / SERVES 4 TO 6

On Sundays, my papa would get up extra early to go on a bike ride. While he was away, my mama would get Vanessa and me ready to go on a hike with my papa once he got back. We would load everything we needed in the Jeep and drive about an hour outside of the city to the hills surrounding our town. I loved these excursions. It made me feel like I was part of the Discovery Channel—my favorite network to watch growing up. Up in those hills, we would search for arrowheads, long lost to their creators, and buried in the soft soil. Vanessa and I often looked for skinny snakes, frogs, and horny toads that we could bring home as new pets. During lunchtime, my papa would find nopales with blooming tunas, or as we know them in the United States, prickly pears or Barbary figs. Tunas are most tender and juicy in the spring months. The texture inside is like a pear, but the flavor is mild and a bit tart, like rhubarb. While teaching Vanessa and me how to light a bonfire, my papa would sit on a nearby rock and use his Swiss army knife to peel the tuna before cutting slices and passing them among us to enjoy.

It's hard to find tunas in the Pacific Northwest, but every once in a while, I am lucky and can find them in Mexican or Asian markets. Tunas come in many colors—green, pink, and sometimes yellow. Whenever I find them, I like to prepare them with fresh yogurt and eat them for breakfast. It's also delicious served with granola and seeds. Additionally, and like any fruit in Mexico, you can eat it fresh with a squeeze of lime and a hint of Tajín (Mexican spicy-sour seasoning salt).

10 large prickly pears
2 cups unsweetened, plain
  Greek yogurt
4 tablespoons honey

To peel the prickly pears, slice both ends off, then make a lengthwise slice about ⅛-inch deep, wedge your fingers underneath the skin, and peel back to remove all the skin at once. Cut the prickly pears into ⅛-inch slices.

Add the yogurt to a bowl, then arrange the sliced prickly pears on top and drizzle with honey or top with your favorite toppings before serving. I like to use a mixture of granola, hemp seeds, or flax seeds.

sopas

Sopa Fria de Pepinos

Cold Cucumber Soup / SERVES 2 TO 4

Léon, the city in Mexico where my family is from, has rainfall only during the summer months of June, July, and August, and the rest of the year, including winter, can be incredibly dry and very hot. So hot that I would often refuse to get in the car after it had been parked in the sun while my mama took us grocery shopping, out of fear that my bare legs would melt into the seats. Our home did not have an air conditioner, and besides having cool wood floors, there was not much we could do to escape the heat. It was usually during those unbearable hot days that my mom would make this soup, and I could not wait to eat it. Cucumbers have cooling properties, and many cultures with hot climates prepare and eat them in dishes that help cool the body down. This recipe is so simple and delicious that it can be made ahead of time and kept in the fridge for a few hours; however, it is best if eaten fresh. My favorite part of this soup is dipping breadsticks into the broth and topping it with fresh mint leaves.

3 cucumbers, peeled, seeded, and cubed
Sea salt
1 (25-ounce) container plain yogurt
1 tablespoon olive oil
1 tablespoon white vinegar
1 tablespoon chopped dill, plus more for garnish
2 cucumbers, sliced into ribbons, for serving
12 mint leaves, chopped
Breadsticks for serving (optional)

Sprinkle the cucumbers with a pinch of salt and wrap in a damp towel for 30 minutes.

In a medium bowl, combine the yogurt, oil, vinegar, and dill. Gently mix.

Rinse the cucumbers with cold water and drain in a colander.

In a blender, combine the cucumbers and the yogurt mixture. Blend well.

Transfer the soup to a container with a lid and place it on the highest shelf of your fridge. Chill for at least 1 hour.

Top the soup with cucumber ribbons, dill, and mint, and serve with a side of breadsticks for dipping.

Sopa Guapa

Attractive Soup / SERVES 4 TO 6

The name of this recipe translates to "attractive soup," a name that I find hilarious to this day. I have yet to understand where the name comes from, but my grandmother Titita Tere always referred to it like that, sopa guapa. Perhaps she named it herself, thinking that the soup was attractive enough to have a corresponding title. Whatever the reason, this is a soup I often refer to myself as "Leftover Soup" because whenever I am at home with no time to hit the grocery store before dinner, I can always count on having these basic ingredients in my fridge: butter, carrots, and eggs. I often made this soup in college, when I wanted something filling and somewhat healthy but wanted to stay on a budget. You can enjoy it topped with sour cream, or warm up some tortillas, roll them into taquitos and dip them into the delicious broth with every spoonful.

4 large carrots, peeled
3 medium tomatoes
2 large hard-boiled
    eggs, peeled
¾ cup (1½ sticks)
    unsalted butter
2 tablespoons chicken
    bouillon powder
Sea Salt
Sour cream, for topping
Toast for serving (optional)

In a large soup pot, combine the whole carrots and 1 cup of water. Bring to a boil for 1 minute, then cook over medium heat for about 10 minutes, or until tender. Drain, reserving the carrots and their cooking liquid separately.

Meanwhile, in a medium skillet, cook the tomatoes over medium heat, without oil, until their skins begin to soften. Drain the tomatoes and remove the skins with a paper towel.

Separate the egg yolks from the egg whites and set aside. Finely dice the whites.

In a blender, combine the carrots and their cooking liquid with the tomatoes and egg yolks. Blend well.

In the same soup pot, melt the butter over medium heat. Add the blended carrot sauce and fry for 5 minutes. Add 5 cups of water and the chicken bouillon powder. Bring the soup to a boil for 5 minutes. Taste and season with salt as needed. Turn off the heat. Lightly mix the egg whites into the soup.

Serve the soup with a dollop of sour cream and a side of warm tortillas.

Sopa de Flor de Calabaza

Squash Blossom Soup / SERVES 4 TO 6

I'm a big fan of edible flowers, including lavender, rose, dandelions, and my favorite, squash blossoms. Mexico grows a variety of squashes, and their blossoms can be enjoyed in many ways. Stuffed and fried, as toppings on salads, or my mom's favorite way of making them—Sopa de Flor de Calabaza. This soup is often served as a side dish, but it's good enough to be the star of the show. So don't hesitate to make an extra batch of tortilla strips, because you will be going back for more.

4 chicken breasts, boneless and skinless

½ medium white onion

3 garlic cloves, divided

4 tablespoons avocado oil, divided

1 teaspoon sea salt

4 corn tortillas, cut into strips

¼ yellow onion, finely chopped

4 cups chopped zucchini

1 cup chopped squash blossoms

1 cup sour cream

In a large soup pot, combine the chicken breasts, white onion, 2 of the garlic cloves, 1 tablespoon of the oil, the salt, and 7 cups of water. Bring everything to a boil for 1 minute, reduce heat to medium, cover, and cook for 15 minutes.

Meanwhile, in a deep skillet, heat the remaining 3 tablespoons of oil over medium-high heat. Fry the tortilla strips until golden brown and crispy. Remove the tortilla strips and cool them on a baking rack lined with paper towels to absorb any excess oil. Do not clean the skillet.

Mince the remaining garlic clove. In the same skillet set over medium-low heat, sauté the yellow onion, zucchini, squash blossoms, and the minced garlic clove in the oil for 8 minutes.

Remove the chicken and save the broth. Shred the chicken with two forks in a bowl.

Using a strainer, strain the chicken broth. Discard the leftover onion and garlic.

Add the broth to the zucchini mixture and cook over medium heat for 5 minutes.

Serve immediately with a dollop of sour cream and the tortilla strips.

Crema de Chile Poblano

Creamy Poblano Soup / SERVES 4 TO 6

This soup seemed very fancy to me as a child, because my mom would reserve it for when she had friends over. I was never allowed to attend these events, so I would pull up a chair to the window that looked into our dining room from the TV room and watch in awe as my mom and her friends chatted the night away. If I was lucky, there would be leftovers of this soup which would become my breakfast the next day. I always prayed there would be leftovers. When I grew up, I learned that this soup is surprisingly simple to make, and now, like my mom, I make it when I want to wow my guests but don't want to spend hours in the kitchen. Garnish with cilantro and queso fresco to make this soup extra creamy and serve it in small bowls before the entrée and you are sure to make an impression.

4 large poblano peppers, seeds removed
¼ cup avocado oil
¼ medium white onion, chopped
6 cups whole milk
4 tablespoons unsalted butter
Sea salt
¼ teaspoon ground black pepper
1 tablespoon cornstarch
Cilantro for serving
Queso fresco for serving

Coarsely chop the poblano peppers and set aside.

In a large soup pot, heat the oil over medium heat. Lightly sauté the peppers and onion until softened but not golden, about 5 minutes.

In a blender, blend the peppers and onions until smooth. Using a strainer, strain the mixture and discard any large chunks.

To the same soup pot, bring the milk to a boil over medium heat. Add the blended peppers and onions and mix well. Reduce the heat to medium-low and simmer the soup for 4 minutes, stirring occasionally. Add the butter and pepper, season with salt, and cook over medium-low heat for 10 minutes. If the soup is too thin, add a cornstarch slurry to thicken it: Dissolve the cornstarch in ½ cup of water and mix into the soup. Serve hot with cilantro and queso fresco.

Crema de Elote

Cream of Corn Soup / SERVES 4 TO 6

This creamy corn soup comes together in less than an hour, and it's sure to be a crowd-pleaser. If dairy is not your thing, I recommend using ghee for butter and cashew milk as an alternative. While most milk alternatives will work, cashew has the closest consistency and taste to dairy milk. If choosing alternative milk, stay away from coconut milk as the taste of coconut will be too strong for the soup and will overpower the true star of the dish, corn.

6 cups whole milk, divided
2 large ears corn, shucked
2 teaspoons chicken bouillon powder
4 tablespoons unsalted butter
Sea salt
2 poblano peppers, roasted, peeled, seeded, and sliced into "rajas" (strips)
Queso panela, cubed

In a large soup pot, bring 5 cups of the milk to a simmer over medium-low heat. Continue simmering for 5 minutes.

Using a sharp knife, cut the corn kernels off the cobs.

In a blender, combine half of the corn kernels and the remaining 1 cup of milk and blend until smooth. Using a strainer, strain the corn mixture into the soup pot. Mix well. Add the remaining corn kernels, the chicken bouillon powder, and the butter. Simmer over medium-low heat for about 10 minutes. Do not overcook as the corn will make the soup too sweet. Season with salt. Serve hot, topped with the rajas and queso panela.

Sopa Verde de Pescado

Green Fish Soup / SERVES 4 TO 6

This mildly spicy fish soup is a common dish in coastal parts of Mexico where fish is fresher and more available than in central parts of Mexico. Because I grew up inland, my family rarely had fish that wasn't canned. Whenever my mom could get her hands on some good-looking and fresh sea bass, she would make this soup for us, a treat that was well received by the entire family. The soup comes together quickly, and as you may have noticed from my other recipes, the secret ingredient is chicken bouillon powder. If I were allowed to have only one spice in my pantry, it would be chicken bouillon—we use it to season everything and it never fails to give the dishes that unique flavor that just says "home."

¼ cup avocado oil

5 Anaheim peppers, seeds removed, and minced

½ medium white onion, minced

1 garlic clove, minced

1 bunch parsley, stems removed and leaves coarsely chopped

1 bunch cilantro, stems removed and leaves coarsely chopped

½ pound sea bass fillet, chopped into ½-inch cubes

2 tablespoons chicken bouillon powder

Sea salt

In a medium soup pot, heat the oil over medium heat. Add the peppers, onion, garlic, parsley, and cilantro and sauté until the peppers and onion begin to soften, 7 to 8 minutes. Add 6 cups of water and the sea bass and bring to a boil over medium-high heat. Add the chicken bouillon powder and mix well. Season with salt as needed. Reduce the heat to low and simmer for 15 minutes. Serve hot.

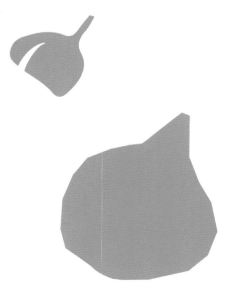

Sopa de Hongos

Mushroom Soup / SERVES 4 TO 6

I love mushrooms and count myself lucky to now be living in the Pacific Northwest, where every fall comes with the tradition of going out into nature in search of wild edible mushrooms. While this is something I never grew up doing in Mexico, my mama was a fan of incorporating mushrooms into our food whenever possible. Mushrooms in tuna salad? Don't knock it until you try it. However, my favorite dish my mom made was this creamy mushroom soup. She would often make this soup during the rainy season when there was a variety of mushrooms available at the market. Which mushrooms you choose is up to you, but I recommend cremini mushrooms for their strong flavor in place of white button mushrooms.

3 tablespoons all-purpose flour

5 cups sliced fresh mushrooms, preferably cremini

4 cups chicken broth

3 tablespoons avocado oil

3 large green onions, white and green parts thinly sliced

3 tablespoons cilantro leaves, chopped

2 teaspoons chicken bouillon powder

In a bowl, combine the flour and 3 cups of water and give it a stir. Add the mushrooms and let them soak for 15 minutes. Drain the mushrooms and set aside.

Meanwhile, in a large soup pot, bring the chicken broth to a simmer over medium heat.

In a medium skillet, heat the oil over medium heat. Add the drained mushrooms and the onions and sauté for 5 minutes until the onions begin to soften and the mushrooms start to brown.

Add the sautéed mushrooms and onions, the cilantro leaves, chicken bouillon powder, and 1 cup of water to the pot of chicken broth and simmer over medium heat for 5 minutes. Serve hot.

Pozole Verde de Pollo

Green Chicken Pozole / SERVES 6 TO 8

Pozole is widely known in the United States and is often ordered by my American friends whenever we go out to a Mexican restaurant. This delicious soup, however, has an origin unknown to most people outside of Mexico. In the Aztec empire, the word "pozole" originates from the Nahuatl language word *pozolli*, which means foam and refers to the frothiness that takes place when you boil corn. Pozole was created in precolonial times as a sacred dish that was consumed by Tlatoani, the ruler or king. When Spanish colonization of Mexico took place, pork was introduced to the dish. Today, pozole can be made with chicken, pork, and even turkey. Similar to chiles en nogada, pozole flavors represent the Mexican flag, and you can find many varieties of pozole rojo (red), pozole verde (green), and pozole blanco (white). There aren't many rules to pozole, except one that I often see broken on American blogs: you do not use crema, sour cream, queso fresco, or any other cheese as a topping. Instead, top with slices of the freshest avocado and radish, and don't forget the squeeze of lime.

2 tablespoons olive oil

½ large white onion, diced

1 serrano pepper, seeds removed, and diced

4 garlic cloves, minced

8 cups chicken broth

3 chicken breasts, boneless and skinless

2 dried bay leaves

2 teaspoons ground cumin

1 teaspoon dried oregano

1 (29-ounce) can hominy, liquid reserved

1 cup Salsa Verde (page 25)

Sea salt and ground black pepper

TOPPINGS

Thinly sliced radishes

Sliced avocado

Lime wedges

Chopped cilantro leaves

Crumbled tortilla chips

In a large soup pot, heat the oil over medium-high heat. Add the onion and pepper and sauté for 3 to 4 minutes. Add the garlic and sauté for 30 seconds. Add the chicken broth, chicken breasts, bay leaves, cumin, and oregano. Bring to a boil over medium-high heat then lower the heat and simmer until the chicken is fully cooked, about 10 minutes.

Carefully remove the chicken from the broth, shred it using two forks, and return it to the pot. Add the hominy and its liquid. Remove and discard the bay leaves. Add up to 1 cup of salsa verde to taste. Cover and simmer the soup over medium-low heat for 30 minutes. Remove from the heat and season with salt and pepper. Serve immediately, topped with radish, avocado, a squeeze of lime, cilantro, and tortilla chips.

Sopa Azteca

Aztec Soup / SERVES 4 TO 6

If I were only allowed to eat one soup for the rest of my life, it would be Sopa Azteca. My mama refers to this soup as levanta muertos (raise the dead), because of the feeling of being reborn after eating it. Sopa Azteca is the perfect comfort food, often a hangover dish that is served for brunch on Sundays. The broth of this soup is rich and spicy with chipotle chiles en adobo, and the toppings are what really make this soup special. I love to load up my bowl with finely diced hard-boiled eggs, a lot of avocado slices, and an impossible amount of tortilla chips that I fry myself. This is a soup that will have you going back for seconds or even thirds.

1 (28-ounce) can tomato sauce

3 canned chipotle peppers in adobo

⅓ medium white onion

2 garlic cloves

6 cups chicken broth

2 chicken breasts, boneless and skinless

2 tablespoons olive oil

Sea salt

1 teaspoon chicken bouillon powder (optional)

1 teaspoon granulated sugar (optional)

TOPPINGS

3 tablespoons avocado oil

15 corn tortillas, cut into 1-inch strips

4 hard-boiled eggs, finely diced

Queso fresco

Sliced avocado

Lime wedges

In a blender, combine the tomato sauce, chipotle peppers, onion, garlic, and 1 cup of water and blend well. Set aside.

In a large soup pot, combine the chicken broth and chicken breasts. Bring to a boil over medium-high heat then lower the heat and simmer until the chicken is fully cooked, about 15 minutes. Carefully remove the chicken from the broth, shred it using two forks, and set aside. Reserve the broth in the pot.

In a large saucepan, heat the olive oil over medium-high heat. Carefully add the tomato sauce mixture, as it will jump in the pan. Lower the heat to medium-low and sauté for about 4 to 5 minutes until the sauce starts to bubble. Add the sauce to the broth in the soup pot and give it a stir. Season with salt and adjust the flavors as needed. If the onion is too sweet, add 1 teaspoon chicken bouillon powder; if the onion is too strong, add 1 teaspoon of sugar to balance the flavors. Add the shredded chicken and simmer over low heat for 10 to 15 minutes.

Meanwhile, in a deep skillet, heat the avocado oil over medium-high heat. Add the tortilla strips and fry until golden and crunchy. Remove the tortillas and set aside on a baking rack lined with paper towels to absorb any excess oil.

Serve the soup immediately, topping each bowl with the hard-boiled eggs, queso fresco, tortilla strips, avocado slices, and lime wedges on the side.

Sopa de Fideo

Mexican Noodle Soup / SERVES 4 TO 6

Children in the United States grow up eating Kraft Macaroni & Cheese. But in Mexico, we have sopa de fideo. Everyone makes this soup a little differently: some on the drier side and some on the soupier side. I prefer mine to be a little gloopy: not too dry and not too brothy. This is a favorite dish among children, but it's a flavor that you never outgrow, and to this day, I find myself craving this soup with a big dollop of sour cream and a side of tortillas for dipping. Additionally, you can top this soup with sour cream, cheese, and avocado slices.

For a heartier pasta dish, do not add the three cups of water when you add the sauce and coriander to the pasta. Allow the pasta to cook until most of the sauce has been absorbed. Serve with your favorite toppings and enjoy!

4 Roma tomatoes, cored

2 canned chipotle peppers in adobo, plus 2 tablespoons adobo sauce

½ medium white onion

2 garlic cloves

2 tablespoons tomato paste

1 teaspoon sea salt

1 tablespoon avocado oil (or olive oil)

3 cups fideo pasta, broken into 2-inch pieces (or angel hair pasta)

½ teaspoon ground coriander

TOPPINGS

Mexican crema or sour cream

Queso fresco

Sliced avocado

Cilantro leaves

In a blender, combine the tomatoes, chipotle peppers and adobo sauce, onion, garlic, tomato paste, salt, and 4 cups of water. Blend until smooth.

In a Dutch oven or heavy-bottomed soup pot, heat the oil over medium-high heat until shimmering. Add the pasta and fry, stirring occasionally, until the pieces turn golden. Add the tomato sauce, coriander, and 3 cups of water. Simmer over medium heat, stirring occasionally to prevent sticking, for about 8 minutes, or until the pasta absorbs as much liquid as possible. Taste and season with salt as needed. Remove from the heat and let the soup rest for about 2 minutes. Serve topped with crema, queso fresco, avocado slices, and cilantro.

Caldo de Verduras

Vegetable Soup / SERVES 4 TO 6

Many families have a version of vegetable soup, a simple and humble dish, with powerful healing properties. Or so it seems, especially when dealing with a cold. Unlike vegetable and chicken soups most kids in the United States eat when they feel sick, this soup uses bacon, providing that delicious fatty flavor, while still allowing vegetables to be the star of the show. My favorite way to eat it is by dipping a fresh piece of sourdough bread, letting the broth bathe the crumb entirely, and taking a bite right before I think the bread might break off into my bowl.

3 slices bacon
2 celery stalks with leaves, coarsely chopped
1 large tomato, coarsely chopped
1 large carrot, peeled and coarsely chopped
½ large white onion, coarsely chopped
1 garlic clove
1 tablespoon olive oil
2 cups fresh spinach leaves
2 tablespoons chicken bouillon powder
Sourdough bread, for serving (optional)

In a cold skillet, add the bacon and cook over medium heat, flipping occasionally, until the bacon has a slight crunch, about 2 to 3 minutes. Remove the bacon before it gets crispy. Set aside on a plate lined with a paper towel.

In a large soup pot, heat oil over medium heat. Combine the celery, tomato, carrot, onion, garlic, and spinach leaves and sauté until the vegetables begin to soften, 5 to 7 minutes. Add the bacon and 7 cups of water and bring to a boil. Reduce the heat to medium-low and simmer for 5 minutes.

In a blender, blend the soup until smooth. Using a strainer, strain the soup and discard any large chunks. Return the soup to the pot and bring to a boil over medium-high heat for 3 minutes. Add the chicken bouillon and mix well. Serve hot with a slice of sourdough bread.

Arroz

Arroz con Huevos Fritos

Rice with Fried Eggs / SERVES 4 TO 6

Similar to tortillas, rice in Mexico is a catch-all starchy bed for many dishes. We love to cook our rice with butter, herbs, vegetables, or stocks. It is rare that we prepare basic plain rice unless using it as a base for a saucy dish like Pollo en Adobo (page 127). This dish, Arroz con Huevos Fritos, was commonly eaten in my house for desayuno, but in college I often ate it as merienda, a late-night snack. My favorite thing to do is to leave the egg yolk kind of runny and mix it with the rice, then add a good amount of hot sauce before combining everything together and eating it by the spoonful.

2 cups dry (uncooked) white, short-grain rice
1 cup avocado oil, plus more for frying
¼ white onion, minced
2 garlic cloves, minced
4 poblano peppers, seeds removed, and coarsely chopped
1 teaspoon chicken bouillon powder
6 large eggs
Chili powder for serving (optional)

Rinse the rice 2 to 3 times with cold water until the water runs clear.

In a large soup pot, heat the oil over medium heat. Add the onion and garlic and sauté until starting to turn golden. Then add the rinsed rice and fry until the grains of rice begin to separate, stirring occasionally to prevent rice from burning. Remove from the heat before the rice turns golden. Drain the oil from the pot.

While the rice is frying, in a blender, combine the peppers and 3 cups of water and blend until smooth. Add to the rice in the soup pot, along with the chicken bouillon powder and 2 cups of water. Mix well with a wooden spoon, cover, and bring to a boil for 1 minute. Reduce heat to simmer and cook, covered, for 20 to 30 minutes, until all the liquid is absorbed.

Meanwhile, add a small amount of oil in a skillet, and fry the eggs.

Serve the rice in bowls with a fried egg on top, dusted with chili powder if you'd like.

Arroz a la Marinera

Seafood Rice / SERVES 4 TO 6

Living in the Pacific Northwest, the fall and winter season can be daunting as the sun begins to set earlier and earlier, sometimes as early as four o'clock. With little to no natural light outside, most nights are spent indoors. That is until I discovered the joy of squidding (fishing for squid). My partner is the one who introduced me to this exciting hobby of putting on headlamps and walking to the water's edge, with buckets in one hand and a small fishing pole in the other. On the docks that make up Seattle's waterfront, you can find crowds of people fishing for squid—primarily Filipino, Korean, and Chinese families. My hometown in Mexico was inland, and the closest I had ever gotten to fresh calamari was only after it had been deep-fried and served to me on a platter at the beach.

I've always had a deep appreciation for foraging, growing, or gathering my own food. So when I found out I could catch more than enough squid to go around, I started to incorporate it into different dishes. My partner is Korean, and he introduced me to a dish called ojingeo deopbap. Adopting his recipe, I decided to start adding squid into a similar rice dish that I grew up eating, made with clams, fish, and shrimp. The beauty of this dish comes from the hard work and love that is put into making it. When making this dish, I recommend sourcing sustainably caught seafood for a result that is not just delicious, but good for communities and the planet.

1½ cups dry (uncooked) white, short-grain rice
3 tablespoons olive oil
3 garlic cloves, minced
1 red bell pepper, sliced into strips
1 green bell pepper, sliced into strips
½ lb calamari (or squid), cleaned
½ lb shrimp, tails on
½ lb red snapper fillet, chopped into 1-inch cubes
1 lb clams, cleaned
1 teaspoon sea salt
1 (15-ounce) can green peas, drained

Rinse the rice 2 to 3 times with cold water until the water runs clear.

In a large soup pot, heat the oil over medium-high heat. Add the rice and garlic and fry, stirring until the grains of rice begin to separate. Drain the oil from the pot. Add the bell peppers, calamari, shrimp, snapper, clams, and 2 ½ cups of water, and mix well. Add the salt and cook over medium-high heat for 15 minutes. Cover, reduce the heat to low, and continue cooking until all the liquid has been absorbed, about 40 minutes. When the rice is ready, the clams should be open; discard any clams that are still closed. Add the green peas and fold them into the rice. Serve hot.

Arroz Blanco con Plátanos Fritos

White Rice with Fried Plantains / SERVES 4 TO 6

This is a dish that can be found across Latin America. Whether it's Cuba, Honduras, or Mexico, you can find variations of this dish topped with tomato sauce, served with carne asada, or decorated with pico de gallo. Try it as a side for your main entrée and pair with a side of black beans.

1½ cups dry (uncooked) white, short-grain rice

6 tablespoons avocado oil

4 garlic cloves, minced

½ lime, juiced and divided

2 tablespoons chicken bouillon powder

8 serrano peppers, chopped (remove seeds for a less spicy salsa)

2 medium tomatoes, finely chopped

½ white onion, finely chopped

3 tablespoons finely chopped cilantro leaves

2 tablespoons olive oil

1 teaspoon sea salt

3 ripe plantains

Rinse the rice 2 to 3 times with cold water until the water runs clear.

In a medium stock pot, heat 3 tablespoons of the avocado oil over medium heat. Add the rice and garlic and fry, stirring occasionally, until the grains of rice begin to separate. Drain the oil from the pot. Add 3 cups of water, ½ teaspoon of the lime juice, and the chicken bouillon powder. Mix well. Cover and bring to a boil for 1 minute. Reduce to simmer and cook until all the liquid has been absorbed, about 30 minutes.

Meanwhile, in a bowl, combine the remaining lime juice, peppers, tomatoes, onion, cilantro, olive oil, and salt. Mix well.

If the plantains are ripe but still a bit hard, roll them on a hard surface, using the heels of your hands to soften them. Peel the plantains and slice into ¼-inch coins.

In a large skillet, heat the remaining 3 tablespoons of avocado oil over medium-high heat. Fry the plantains until golden brown, about 2 minutes on each side.

Serve the rice in bowls, topped with salsa, and serve with fried plantains.

Arroz Rojo

Red Rice / SERVES 4 TO 6

Red rice is a staple in Mexican cuisine and served with the majority of platos fuertes (entrées). The flavor and color of the rice comes from puréed tomatoes. For best results, pick tomatoes that are very ripe and the deepest shades of red. Traditionally, some households like to add vegetables to the rice, such as corn, peas, or finely chopped carrots. If you wish to take this approach, use about ½ cup of each vegetable and add to the rice at the same time as the tomato salsa. This rice is delicious served as a side with many dishes, but my favorite is Chiles Rellenos (page 42).

1½ cups dry (uncooked) white, short-grain rice
4 Roma tomatoes, cores removed
½ white onion, chopped
2 tablespoons olive oil
1 garlic clove, minced
1 teaspoon sea salt

Rinse the rice 2 to 3 times with cold water until the water runs clear.

In a blender, combine the tomatoes, onion, and ½ cup of water. Blend until smooth. The mixture should make about 2 cups of salsa. Top off the salsa with additional water if needed to make 2 cups.

In a medium saucepan, heat the oil over medium heat. Add the rice and garlic and fry, stirring constantly, until the grains of rice begin to separate. Add the tomato salsa and salt and bring to a boil. Boil for 1 minute then lower the heat, cover, and simmer undisturbed until all the liquid has been absorbed, about 15 minutes. After 15 minutes, check the rice for tenderness—the grains should be tender and easy to separate but not mushy. Cook for 2 to 5 minutes more as needed until the rice has the desired texture. Serve warm with your favorite dishes.

Arroz a la Jardinera

Gardener's Rice / SERVES 4 TO 6

"Jardin" in Spanish translates to backyard or garden. The name of this dish comes from all the vegetables that you might find in a garden, perhaps your own. Which vegetables you add is entirely up to you. However, this recipe uses the vegetables I most commonly ate when my mama made this dish. Additionally, you can add canned sweet corn, and even very finely diced pre-baked potatoes right after the zucchini for a more substantial meal.

1½ cups dry (uncooked) white, short-grain rice
6 tablespoons avocado oil
2 large tomatoes, chopped
¼ white onion, chopped
2 garlic cloves, chopped
8 green beans, halved lengthwise
½ cup green peas
1 green bell pepper, sliced into strips
1 red bell pepper, sliced into strips
3 carrots, peeled and chopped
3 zucchinis, chopped
2 tablespoons chicken bouillon powder

Rinse the rice 2 to 3 times with cold water until the water runs clear.

In a large soup pot, heat 3 tablespoons of the oil over medium-high heat. Add the rice and fry without stirring for 3 to 5 minutes. Remove from the heat and drain the oil from the pot.

In a blender, combine the tomatoes, onion, and garlic. Blend until smooth. Using a strainer, strain the mixture. Set aside.

In a skillet, heat the remaining 3 tablespoons of oil over medium heat. Add the green beans and green peas and sauté until they start to soften. Remove from the heat and set aside.

Place the pot of rice over medium-high heat. Add the bell peppers and carrots and give it a stir. Reduce the heat to medium and cook for 3 minutes. Add the tomato mixture and cook, stirring occasionally with a wooden spoon, for 5 minutes. Add the zucchinis, chicken bouillon powder, and 2½ cups of hot water. Mix well, cover, and cook over medium-low heat until all the liquid has been absorbed, about 40 minutes. A few minutes before the rice is ready, fold in the green beans and green peas. Serve hot.

Harinas

Sopes

Fried Masa Bowls / SERVES 4 TO 6

Sopes are the best Mexican appetizer. Because the dough is fried, they maintain their shape, making them perfect little bowls that you can fill up and pass around. The most traditional way to eat them is topped with refried beans, Mexican sour cream, shredded lettuce, sliced radish, and a sprinkle of queso fresco. You can add your favorite salsa to give them a little kick. Sopes are made from the same masa as tortillas. If you have access to fresh masa near you, I highly recommend going that route; otherwise, you can easily find Maseca flour, which requires you to add only water to form the perfect dough. You could also make these sopes the main dish, by making them slightly larger and topping them with shredded chicken or carnitas.

1 cup Maseca flour

3 cups avocado oil, divided

4 dried poblano peppers,
    seeds removed

2½ teaspoons sea salt, divided

1 garlic clove

4 medium Roma tomatoes

½ teaspoon dried oregano

½ pound skirt steak

½ teaspoon Montreal steak
    seasoning

TOPPINGS

Refried beans (page 51)

Shredded iceberg lettuce

Mexican crema or sour cream

Crumbled queso fresco

Sliced radishes

In a medium bowl, combine the Maseca flour with ½ cup of water and mix with your hands or a wooden spoon. Mix in an additional ½ cup of water until a smooth dough is formed. Knead the dough with your hands and form a ball.

Divide the dough into 6 small balls. Pat down each ball to create a flat circle of dough that is 4 inches in diameter. These are your sopes.

In a large pan, heat 2 cups of the oil over medium-high heat. Working in batches, fry the sopes, turning frequently, until golden, about 5 minutes. Remove from pan and pat down with a paper towel.

Carefully shape the sopes by pinching the sides of the circles to create shallow bowls. Set aside to cool.

In a small pot, combine the dried poblano peppers with enough cold water to cover them, and bring to a boil over medium-high heat. Drain the peppers, reserving 1 cup of the cooking liquid.

In a blender, combine the peppers, the 1 cup of reserved liquid, 1 teaspoon of salt, and the garlic. Blend until smooth. Set aside in a shallow bowl.

In the same small pot, combine the tomatoes with enough water to cover them and 1 teaspoon of salt. Bring to a boil over medium-high heat.

RECIPE CONTINUES ⟶

Sopes / Fried Masa Bowls

Reduce the heat to medium and cook until the skins of the tomatoes begin to split. Drain the tomatoes, reserving ½ cup of the cooking liquid.

In a blender, combine the tomatoes, the reserved ½ cup liquid, the pepper sauce, oregano, and ½ teaspoon of salt. Blend until smooth. Set aside.

Heat a large pan over medium-high heat. Add the steak seasoning to both sides of the steak. Sear the steak, flipping occasionally, for 8 to 10 minutes, or until medium-rare. Transfer the steak to a cutting board and slice into thin strips.

In a large pan, heat the remaining 1 cup of oil over medium-high heat. Dip the sopes in the tomato sauce so they are covered on both sides. Fry the sauce-dipped sopes, flipping frequently, for 4 to 5 minutes. Place the sopes on a baking rack lined with paper towels to remove any excess oil.

Meanwhile, heat the refried beans over low heat in a small saucepan.

To serve, add some refried beans to the base of each sope. Top with the carne asada, lettuce, Mexican crema, sliced radishes, and queso fresco.

Crepas de Espinacas con Queso

Spinach and Cheese Crepes / SERVES 4 TO 6

My Tita Maru used to make these crepes on special occasions, whether it was a cousin's primera comunión, Easter, or a birthday. Whatever the occasion, I remember never being able to eat enough of these Crepas de Espinacas con Queso before they ran out. I love crepes for their versatility—they are the perfect vessels for either savory or sweet flavors. If you want to take these crepes up a level, I recommend serving them with sliced avocado and hot sauce.

1 tablespoon avocado oil

1 slice bacon, finely chopped

½ white onion, finely chopped

2 cups rinsed and chopped spinach

3 tablespoons chopped pecans

Sea salt

1 packet (10 to 12) premade crepes

FOR THE BÉCHAMEL

4 tablespoons unsalted butter (or margarine)

4 tablespoons all-purpose flour

3 cups whole milk, warm

Sea salt and ground black pepper

⅔ cup grated medium cheddar cheese

Preheat the oven to 300°F. Grease a 9x13-inch glass baking dish with butter.

In a medium skillet, heat the oil over medium heat and add the bacon. Once the bacon begins to brown, add the onion, and cook until it's translucent. Add the spinach and pecans and mix. Cover, reduce the heat to medium-low, and cook until the liquid from the spinach has been completely absorbed, about 5 minutes. Season with salt, remove from the heat and keep warm.

Make the Béchamel

In a heavy-bottomed saucepan, melt the butter over medium-low heat. Add the flour and stir constantly. Cook until the paste begins to bubble, but don't let it brown, about 2 minutes. Add the milk and continue to stir as the sauce thickens. Bring the sauce to a boil over medium-high heat. Season with salt and pepper. Reduce the heat to low and cook, stirring, for 2 to 3 minutes. Remove from the heat.

Place 3 tablespoons of the spinach mixture on the end of a crepe. Roll it up like a burrito. Repeat the process, arranging the crepes, edge-side down and side by side, in the greased baking dish. Bathe the crepes in the béchamel and top with the cheese. Bake for 15 minutes, or until the cheese has melted. Serve hot.

Enchiladas

SERVES 4 TO 6

There are so many variations of enchiladas in Mexico: enchiladas rojas, suizas, enchiladas de mole—the list goes on and on. What is most important about enchiladas are the filling and the sauce. Traditionally, enchiladas are filled with chicken, but if you want a vegetarian option, you can fill them with roasted vegetables such as zucchini, corn, mushrooms, and, of course, a deliciously melty cheese. Enjoy the enchiladas topped with sour cream, queso fresco, and chopped fresh cilantro.

1 white onion
4 chicken breasts, skinless and boneless
3 garlic cloves
2 pounds ripe tomatoes, chopped
½ cup plus 1 tablespoon avocado oil
2 teaspoons smoked paprika
2 teaspoons ground cumin
2½ teaspoons chicken bouillon powder
18 corn tortillas
⅔ cup grated Manchego cheese

TOPPINGS (OPTIONAL)
Sour cream
Queso fresco
Cilantro leaves

Preheat the oven to 350°F and grease a 9x13-inch pan.

Chop three-quarters of the onion and set aside. Cut the remaining quarter into 4 pieces.

In a large stockpot over medium-high heat, combine the 4 pieces of onion, the chicken breasts, garlic, and 5 cups of cold water. Bring to a boil for 1 minute, then cover with a lid, lower the heat to medium-low, and cook for 20 minutes.

In a blender, combine the reserved chopped onion and the tomatoes and blend well.

Meanwhile, in a large skillet, heat the ½ cup of oil over medium heat. Add the blended tomato sauce, paprika, and cumin, and give it a stir. Simmer, uncovered, over medium-low heat until the oil begins to separate, and the sauce begins to thicken, about 15 minutes.

Carefully remove the chicken from the pot, shred it using two forks, and set aside.

Using a strainer, strain the chicken liquid from the pot, reserving 1 cup. Add the reserved 1 cup of chicken liquid and the chicken bouillon powder to the tomato sauce. Mix well.

Add 1 cup of the tomato sauce to the shredded chicken. Stir until the chicken is fully covered.

In a large skillet, heat the remaining 1 tablespoon of oil over medium heat. One at a time, gently fry the tortillas until flexible, about 1 minute. Remove the tortillas from the oil before they harden. You don't want crispy tostadas or chips.

Make small taquitos with the tortillas. Add 2 tablespoons of the chicken mixture to the center of a tortilla and roll it up. Repeat the process and arrange the taquitos, edge-side down and side by side, in the greased pan. Bathe the taquitos in the remaining tomato sauce and top with the Manchego cheese. Bake for 20 minutes, or until the cheese is golden and bubbly. Serve hot, topped with a dollop of sour cream, queso fresco, and cilantro, if using.

Tortas Guacamayas

Macaw Sandwiches / SERVES 4 TO 6

While tacos are the most-known Mexican dish outside of Mexico, in Mexico tortas are just as popular and mouthwatering. Much like tacos, tortas are a vessel to get food from your plate into your mouth, and it doesn't really matter what you put inside, as long as the bread is a bolillo roll, or something as close as possible. Bolillos are crunchy on the outside with a tender and soft crumb. A good alternative is to find really nice French rolls. What you put inside is entirely up to you. Tortas guacamayas are a regional dish only to be found in my hometown of León, Guanajuato. No matter how you might search for them anywhere else, this is the only city that will make them and serve them. Their name was inspired by the resemblance of the ingredients' colors to those of a macaw. Each torta is filled with crispy chicharrón, spicy pico de gallo, and a squeeze of fresh lime; avocado slices can be added if you like. It's impossible to finish one without wanting another one almost immediately.

FOR THE PICO DE GALLO
3 medium Roma tomatoes, diced
2 serrano peppers, diced
½ large white onion, chopped
1 cup chopped cilantro leaves

FOR THE SALSA
1 medium Roma tomato, halved lengthwise
2 chile de árbol peppers, stems removed
½ large white onion, diced
1 garlic clove
1 tablespoon lime juice, plus more to taste
Sea salt and freshly ground black pepper

FOR THE TORTAS
4 to 6 bolillo rolls (or French rolls)
2 cups original flavor (or lightly salted) pork rinds
2 limes, sliced into wedges
Verduras en Escabeche, optional (page 33)
Avocado slices (optional)

Make the Pico de Gallo
In a medium bowl, combine the tomatoes, serrano peppers, and onion. Gently mix in the cilantro. Place the pico de gallo in the fridge until ready to use.

Make the Salsa
In a skillet, roast the halved tomatoes, skin-side down, over medium heat until the skins begin to soften, crack, and slightly char. Add the árbol peppers, onion, and garlic and cook for 5 to 7 minutes. Transfer to a blender, and slowly blend with ½ cup of water, adding more water until you have a smooth salsa.

In a medium bowl, mix the salsa with the pico de gallo. Add the lime juice and season with salt and pepper. Set aside.

Make the Tortas
Toast the rolls for a few minutes until the outer layer is golden and crunchy. Split the rolls in half. Remove the soft, inner crumb layer (also known as the belly of the bread) from both sides of each roll. Top one half of a roll with pork rinds. Add salsa avocado (if using) and top with the second half of the roll. Repeat the process and serve with lime wedges on the side. For an extra kick, serve with Verduras en Escabeche.

Tamales

SERVES 6 TO 8

I used to be really intimidated by the thought of making tamales. It seemed like a daunting and difficult task reserved for the holidays. As I grew older, I was invited to partake in the process and learned that there isn't any special technical skill required to make delicious tamales. Making tamales with my mom has become one of my favorite traditions. Because the process is lengthy, the time is usually spent with chismes (gossip), stories, and lots of laughter. Before we know it, we have wrapped all of our masa in corn husks and our little bundles are ready for their steam bath. In Mexico there are two ways to wrap your tamales: in corn husks and in banana leaves. But in my family we always use corn husks, as they are more available in the United States. If you are making a big batch, you can reserve some of the masa for sweet tamales. Instead of being filled with meat, they are sprinkled with raisins and filled with fruit or cajeta (dulce de leche) and pecans.

TOOLS
30-quart tamale steamer pot

FOR THE FILLING
¾ pound chicken breasts,
    boneless and skinless
2 thick onion slices (from
    about ¼ onion)
2 garlic cloves
3 cups Salsa Verde (page 25)

FOR THE TAMALES
45 corn husks
1¾ cups lard
5 cups Maseca flour
6 cups chicken broth
1 teaspoon baking powder
Sea salt

FOR THE TOPPINGS
(OPTIONAL)
Mexican crema or sour cream
Salsa Verde (page 25)
Queso fresco

Make the Filling

In a large soup pot, combine the chicken, onion, garlic, and 5 cups of water. Bring to a boil, and after 1 minute, reduce heat to medium-high heat and cook until the chicken is fully cooked, about 20 minutes. Carefully remove the chicken from the pot, shred it using two forks, and let cool.

Add the salsa verde to the shredded chicken. Set aside.

Make the Tamales

In a large dish filled with hot water, soak the corn husks to make them softer and more flexible, about 30 minutes.

Meanwhile, in a stand mixer, whip the lard until it's almost transparent. Slowly add the Maseca flour in small batches. Add the chicken broth and baking powder. Mix well and season with salt. Continue to mix until the dough is light and spongy.

Assemble the Tamales

Dry the softened husks with a soft cloth or paper towel.

Place the husks on a work surface with the wider end toward you. Spread 2 tablespoons of dough in the center of each husk, closer to the wider edge.

Add 2 tablespoons of the chicken. Fold one long side of the husk towards the center and fold the other side in the same manner. Take the skinny end of the husk (the edge farthest from you) and fold it toward the center. One end of each tamale will be closed and one will be open. Repeat until you are out of dough and chicken; you should have leftover corn husks. Set the tamales aside on a tray.

Put 3 cups of hot water in the tamale pot. Place the steaming rack inside. Use the leftover corn husks to create a base layer on the rack. Gently arrange the tamales vertically in the pot with the wider end on the bottom and the narrow end facing the top. Cover the tamales with another layer of corn husks and a kitchen towel.

Cover with a lid and steam the tamales over medium heat for 60 minutes. Check your tamales; they are ready when the masa dough easily peels away from the corn husk. Be careful not to burn yourself. Remove the pot from the heat.

Let the tamales rest in the pot for 10 minutes. Serve warm. You can serve the tamales topped with salsa, sour cream, and queso fresco.

Enfrijoladas

Bean Enchiladas / SERVES 4 TO 6

I grew up eating enfrijoladas at least a few times per month. Enfrijoladas are essentially enchiladas, but with a silky bean sauce that will have you going back for more. It's hard for me to stop eating these once I start, and I can often eat four before my self-control kicks in. Enjoy these topped with crema, queso fresco, and shredded lettuce, and if you want to make them the way my papa likes, top with Salsa Verde (page 25).

2 dried guajillo peppers (or 2 dried California peppers), seeds removed

1 dried ancho pepper, seeds removed

3 tablespoons avocado oil

1 small white onion, chopped

2 serrano peppers, sliced

2 garlic cloves, minced

½ teaspoon ground cumin

½ teaspoon smoked paprika

3 cups canned black beans, with their liquid

2 cups chicken stock, plus more as needed

Sea salt

12 corn tortillas

TOPPINGS

Sour cream

Crumbled queso fresco

Shredded iceberg lettuce

1 cup cooked shredded chicken (optional)

In a medium saucepan, combine the guajillo and ancho peppers and 2 cups of water. Bring to a boil, then after 1 minute, lower the heat to medium heat and simmer until the peppers are soft, 7 to 8 minutes. Drain the peppers and set aside.

In a large saucepan, heat 1 tablespoon of the oil over medium heat. Add the onion and sauté for 5 minutes. Add the serrano peppers, garlic, cumin, paprika, the beans and their liquid, and the chicken stock. Season with salt. Simmer for 3 to 5 minutes.

In a blender, combine the peppers and the bean mixture. Pulse into a smooth sauce. Return to the same large saucepan and cook over medium-low heat for 5 minutes. If your sauce is too thick, slowly add more chicken stock. Transfer the sauce to a bowl.

In a large skillet, heat the remaining 2 tablespoons of oil over medium-high heat. One by one, fry the tortillas, flipping once, until softened. You want flexible tortillas, not crispy tostadas. Set the fried tortillas on a paper towel to absorb any excess oil.

Soak each fried tortilla in the bean sauce and roll them up. Serve on a plate, topped with sour cream, queso fresco, and shredded lettuce. And if you'd like, you can dip the tortillas in the bean sauce and fill with shredded chicken before rolling.

Chilaquiles

SERVES 4 TO 6

Reimagining and eating a plate of stale tortillas probably doesn't sound very appetizing, but wait until you try chilaquiles. Old tortillas get a second life by being cut into wedges, fried to a golden crisp, then softened in a rich salsa and topped with my favorite garnishes. I modified this recipe so it's extra quick to make, supplementing the tortillas with tortilla chips. If going this route, select high-quality tortilla chips that are thick and crispy—otherwise, you will end up with a sloppy mess instead of chilaquiles. To me, chilaquiles are the equivalent of fried rice—it's the dish you make for desayuno, repurposing all of last night's leftovers. Tortillas, salsa, crema, queso fresco, and whatever else you have at hand. If I am eating them for breakfast, I often like to add a sunny-side-up egg on top, or chopped chorizo, and serve with a side of beans; for lunch or dinner you can add carne asada or chicken.

2 tablespoons avocado oil
Salsa Roja (page 26)
1 (24-ounce) bag tortilla chips
⅔ cup shredded Manchego cheese
⅓ cup crumbled Cotija cheese (or queso fresco)
3 to 4 radishes, thinly sliced
½ cup chopped cilantro leaves
¼ cup chopped red onion (optional)
1 ripe avocado, thinly sliced

In a large skillet, heat the oil over medium heat; the oil is ready when a light sprinkle of flour sizzles on contact. Add the salsa roja and simmer over medium-low heat for about 5 minutes. Add the tortilla chips. Using a flexible spatula, gently toss until all the chips are coated in the sauce. Top with the Manchego cheese, reduce the heat, cover, and cook until the cheese is melted. For a crunchier chip, continue to cook the chilaquiles for 5 to 7 additional minutes. Remove from the heat. Test a chip to see if it has softened to your liking.

Scoop onto individual plates and serve with a generous amount of Cotija cheese, radishes, cilantro, and red onion, if using. Top with avocado slices and serve immediately.

Torta de Elote

Corn Cake / SERVES 6 TO 8

We can assume everyone in America knows about cornbread, and believe me, I love cornbread. But Torta de Elote is a whole new version I bet you haven't tried before. While cornbread is crumbly and a bit dry until it's blanketed in warm butter, torta de elote is sticky and perfectly versatile. In this recipe, I opted for the more traditional way of eating it, which is alongside Carne de Puerco con Rajas en Salsa de Tomate (page 134). The cake is served with a bath of sauce, a slice of queso fresco, a raja (roasted poblano pepper strip), and sour cream. The sweetness of the corn cake pairs perfectly with the savoriness of the pork, creating a harmony of flavors that ties the two dishes together. The leftovers of this cake go perfectly alongside a cup of black coffee the next morning.

4 medium ears white corn

4 medium eggs

1 (9.9-ounce) can sweetened condensed milk, plus more for thinning the batter

½ cup (1 stick) unsalted butter, melted

1 tablespoon baking powder

2 cups all-purpose flour, plus more as needed

Preheat the oven to 350°F. Grease a Bundt cake pan with butter and dust with flour to prevent the cake from sticking. Alternatively, use nonstick baking spray in place of the butter and flour.

Husk the corn, removing any lingering corn silk, and use a knife to remove all the kernels.

In a blender, combine the corn kernels, eggs, sweetened condensed milk, and melted butter. Blend until smooth; some of the corn kernels will not be fully blended. Add the baking powder and slowly add the flour, ¼ cup at a time, blending until each addition is fully incorporated before adding the next. The batter should have a slightly thicker consistency than pancake batter. If your batter is too loose, add more flour, ¼ cup at a time, until the ideal consistency is achieved; if your batter is too thick, add more sweetened condensed milk, 2 tablespoons at a time, until you reach a consistency like pancake batter.

Add batter to the greased pan and bake for 40 to 50 minutes, or until a butter knife comes out clean.

Let the cake cool completely before attempting to remove it.

Serve cold or warm, alongside Carne de Puerco con Rajas en Salsa de Tomate, with a slice of queso fresco on top, a dollop of sour cream, a bath of sauce, and rajas.

TIP: This cake is also great as a dessert if you add a 1½ teaspoons of ground cinnamon to the batter.

Empanadas de Pescado

Fried Fish Turnovers / SERVES 4 TO 6

Empanadas are a classic Mexican to-go food. They can be found fresh from street vendors and in restaurants, but there is nothing better than a homemade empanada. Anything can go inside an empanada. During the weekday, my mama would make "Hawaiian" empanadas filled with melty cheese, cubed Spam meat, and sliced pineapple. When I was younger, my favorite empanadas could only be found on Mexico's Pacific coast, in Puerto Vallarta. There was nothing that said vacation more than sitting on the beach facing the ocean with a plate of dogfish (a type of small shark) empanadas, which were my favorite growing up. Since dogfish is less commonly eaten in the United States, I have modified the recipe to be used with cod or other similar white fish. You can serve them as the main dish alongside a salad like Ensalada de Calabacitas (page 37) or make a smaller size and bring a batch of them to a party and serve them as appetizers.

6 medium cod fillets (or rockfish or swordfish fillets)

Juice of 1 lime

4 Roma tomatoes

4 tablespoons olive oil

1 white onion, chopped

2 garlic cloves, minced

Chiffonade of 4 epazote leaves (or 2 tablespoons chopped cilantro leaves)

1 cup evaporated milk

5 strips pickled jalapeño, chopped

12 cups Maseca flour

1 tablespoon all-purpose flour

1 cup avocado oil

Gently rinse the fish with cold water, then place in a bowl with enough cold water to submerge them, plus a few drops of lime juice. Let the fish soak for 10 minutes, then drain and gently pat dry with a paper towel.

Meanwhile, bring a medium saucepan full of water to a boil. Add the tomatoes and boil for about 1 minute, or until their skins begin to crack. Carefully remove the tomatoes from the water and peel them with a paper towel. Slice the tomatoes in half, remove the seeds with a spoon, and chop into ½-inch cubes.

Add 3 tablespoons of the olive oil to a large skillet over medium-high heat. Add the tomatoes, onion, garlic, and epazote and sauté, making sure the tomato cubes do not get too mushy. After 3 minutes, add the evaporated milk and the fish fillets. Reduce the temperature to low and simmer for 10 minutes, or until almost all the juices have evaporated. Remove from the heat. Shred the fish with two forks inside the skillet, add the pickled jalapeño, and gently stir to incorporate everything.

In a medium bowl, combine the Maseca flour with the all-purpose flour, the remaining 1 tablespoon of olive oil, and 2 tablespoons of water. Mix together with your hands until fully incorporated. With your hands, form the dough into balls the size of a small lemon. Using a tortilla press, or your hands and two sheets of parchment paper, flatten each ball into a disk. Place 2 or 3 tablespoons of the fish stew in each disk and fold in half like a quesadilla, sealing the edges with your fingers. You can use a little bit of water on the edges to help the dough stick together. Using a fork, gently press down on the edges to create a design.

In a large, deep skillet, heat the avocado oil until hot but not smoking. Working in batches of three, fry the empanadas, flipping, until the edges begin to look golden brown, about 2 minutes per side. Place a paper towel on a cooling rack and allow the empanadas to rest there after frying to remove any excess oil.

Serve hot.

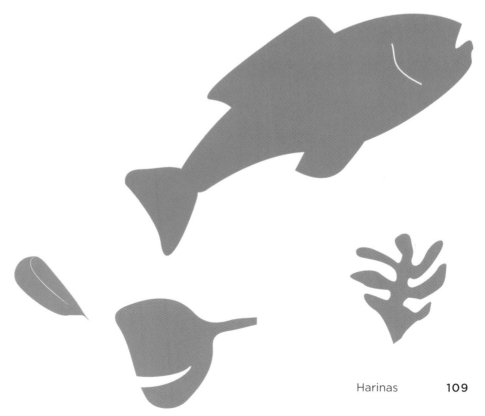

Molletes

Open-Faced Bean Sandwich / SERVES 4

This is a typical breakfast for kids and students, or sometimes a snack for merienda. Bolillo rolls get sliced in half, then half the crumb is removed and replaced with a thin layer of melted butter and Frijoles Refritos (page 51), covered in melty cheese, and topped with Pico de Gallo (page 29) or your salsa of choice. Top these Molletes with chorizo, shredded chicken, or carnitas for a heartier meal.

4 bolillo rolls (or French rolls)
Unsalted butter, room temperature
1 cup Frijoles Refritos (page 51)
1 cup shredded Chihuahua cheese, mozzarella, or sharp cheddar
1 cup Pico de Gallo (page 29)

Preheat the broiler on low and move an oven rack to a few inches below the top of the oven.

Line a baking sheet with parchment paper.

Slice each bolillo roll in half. Remove some crumb from each of the halves, and spread butter on each side. Spread frijoles refritos on each side, top with a generous amount of cheese, and place on the cookie sheet. Broil for 3 to 5 minutes, or until the cheese is melted and bubbly. Do not walk away from your broiler as you might accidentally burn the bread. Serve warm topped with pico de gallo.

WHERE ARE THE TACOS?

I didn't intend to exclude tacos. As the cookbook came together, I considered adding a few taco recipes but hesitated. Here's the truth about tacos: If you want to eat a taco like a Mexican immigrant, you don't need a recipe. As Chef Gabriela Camara said in her book, *My Mexico City Kitchen*, "Everything can be a taco," and she's right.

Growing up, my mom would melt a ridiculous amount of butter on a tortilla, adding cinnamon sugar before rolling it up into the perfect snack. After school, I would rush home to the fridge, slap sour cream and salt on a tortilla, roll it up, and eat it as fast as I could before my parents could catch me. Almost all dishes in Mexico, from breakfast to dinner, are served with a side of tortillas. A taco is much less a meal than it is a vessel to get your favorite foods from your plate into your mouth.

In Mexico, there are few rules regarding tacos. However, once you hold a taco in your hand, you must never let it go. If you put the taco down before you finish eating, it will fall apart. On the other hand, if you're holding onto a hard shell, you're not eating a taco. If your tortilla is as crispy as it is crunchy, you are eating a tostada.

Almost anything in this cookbook can be a taco. All you need is a side of tortillas. If you want to roll up your Plátanos con Crema (page 164) or Arroz con Leche (page 161) inside a tortilla, I will not judge you. Pollo en Adobo (page 127)? Perfect. Sopa de Fideo (page 75)? I can't wait for you to try this! Spread sour cream and a pinch of salt onto a tortilla; dip it into the broth and tell me you don't like what you taste. So, a darle que es mole de olla! (Dig in, it's time to eat!)

Carnes

Albondigas en Chipotle

Meatballs in Chipotle Sauce / SERVES 4 TO 6

In Mexico, work hours are different than in the United States. Instead of working nine to five with a thirty-minute or hour lunch break, Mexico—a country that revolves around the next meal—has a scheduled block of two hours around three o'clock in the afternoon when people go home for comida (a midday meal that is spent with family, and the equivalent of dinner), then head back to work for another few hours before returning home around eight o'clock in the evening. This was my papa's schedule when I was a kid. On special nights, he would return home to surprise my sister and me with a rented VHS tape. I remember the night he brought home *The Lady and the Tramp*. Not only did my sister Vanessa and I both love this movie, but it was also the first time we ever saw meatballs served with spaghetti instead of rice. Traditionally albondigas are served in soup, but my mama preferred to serve them dry over rice or potatoes, topped with salsa. Eating albondigas takes me back to a simpler time, sitting on the floor with Vanessa, watching two dogs kiss over a plate of meatballs and stringy noodles.

FOR THE MEATBALLS
¼ cup all-purpose flour, plus more as needed
½ pound ground beef
½ pound ground pork
2 tablespoons finely chopped onion
1 garlic clove, minced
2 teaspoons finely chopped parsley leaves
2 teaspoons panko breadcrumbs
½ teaspoon sea salt
¼ teaspoon ground black pepper
2 large eggs
¼ cup plus 2 tablespoons avocado oil

FOR THE SALSA
5 dried chipotle peppers, seeded
3 large tomatoes, halved
2 tablespoons finely chopped white onion
1 garlic clove, minced
1 tablespoon tomato purée
2 tablespoons avocado oil
Sea salt

Cooked rice for serving (optional)
Mashed potatoes for serving (optional)

Make the Meatballs

Place the flour in a shallow bowl.

In a large bowl, combine the remaining meatball ingredients, except the oil and mix with your hands. Make chestnut-sized 1-inch balls out of the meat mixture. Roll the meatballs in the flour and set aside.

In a deep skillet, heat the 6 tablespoons of oil over medium-high heat. Briefly sear the meatballs until they turn golden brown. Set aside.

Make the Salsa

In a dry skillet over medium heat, lightly roast the chipotle peppers. Transfer to a soup pot, add 2 cups of water, and bring to a boil. Cook the peppers until they soften, 5 to 7 minutes. Drain the peppers, reserving 1 cup of the cooking liquid. Set aside.

In a blender, combine the softened peppers, the reserved 1 cup of cooking liquid, the tomatoes, onion, garlic, and tomato purée. Blend until smooth.

In a stockpot, heat the 2 tablespoons of oil over medium heat. Add the blended sauce and fry for 3 to 5 minutes. Add the meatballs and 1½ cups of cold water. Bring to a boil for 1 minute, then cover with a lid and simmer over medium-low heat for 15 minutes. Season with salt. Serve with rice or mashed potatoes.

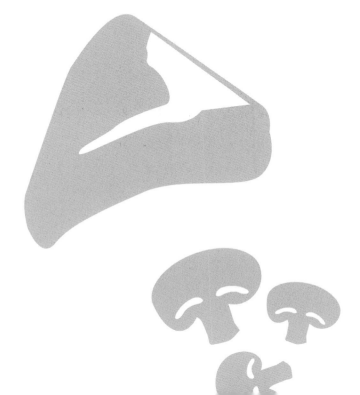

Picadillo

Meat and Vegetable Hash / SERVES 4 TO 6

Picadillo is a dish that made its way all around Latin America and the Philippines due to the Spanish colonization of these various countries. From Mexico to Cuba and the Philippines, we all have a version of picadillo. The one constant is the ground beef and pork that goes into the base of the dish. Traditionally, picadillo is scooped up with a tortilla and eaten as a taco. You can serve it with rice and a side of black beans; place everything inside the tortilla and top with crema! If you are looking for a low-carb option, enjoy it as is or with a side of baked sweet potatoes.

3 tablespoons olive oil

⅓ medium white onion, chopped

2 garlic cloves, minced

1 pound ground beef

1 pound ground pork

1 cup chopped smoked bacon

1 large potato, cut into small cubes

1 tablespoon Maggi sauce

2 dried bay leaves

1 teaspoon dried marjoram

1 teaspoon dried thyme

2 tablespoons chicken bouillon powder

2 tablespoons capers, with their brine

1 zucchini, chopped

1 large carrot, chopped

12 green olives, pitted and halved lengthwise

Sea salt and freshly ground black pepper

Cooked white, short-grain rice for serving (optional)

Warm corn tortillas for serving (optional)

Mashed potatoes or mashed sweet potatoes for serving (optional)

In a large skillet, heat the oil over medium heat. Add the onion and garlic and sauté until the onions are aromatic. Add the beef, pork, bacon, potato, Maggi sauce, dried herbs, chicken bouillon powder, and ½ cup of water. Give it a stir, cover, and cook until the meat turns brown, about 15 minutes. Add the capers, plus some of the brine, along with the zucchini, carrot, and olives. Mix well. Add a bit more water as needed, so the vegetables have enough liquid to steam. Cover and simmer over medium-low heat for 8 minutes, or until the liquid has reduced and the vegetables are tender. Remove from the heat but keep covered for 5 minutes, so the meat can absorb all the juices. Season with salt and pepper.

Serve with a side of mashed potatoes or rice and warm tortillas.

Carne de Puerco Empanizada

Breaded Pork Loin Chops / SERVES 4 TO 6

Also known as milanesas, these breaded pork chops are considered a plato fuerte in Mexico, translating to literally "a strong dish," which is what we call our entrée. This dish is served with potatoes, a fresh salad of greens, tomatoes, and onion, or sometimes served with rice and beans, but always with a squeeze of lime juice on top. When I ate this meal as a kid, my mom would make it with mashed potatoes, and if there were any leftovers the next day, I usually showed up at school with a milanesa torta! Try it yourself by spreading refried beans on a bolillo roll or French roll, adding avocado slices, crema, a milanesa, and topping it with your favorite salsa.

1 cup panko breadcrumbs
½ teaspoon smoked paprika
Sea salt and ground black
    pepper
1 large egg
6 pork loin chops, flattened
    to ½-inch thickness
¼ cup avocado oil
Lime wedges for serving
Chopped cilantro leaves for
    serving

In a medium bowl, mix the breadcrumbs, paprika, and a pinch of black pepper. Season with salt.

Place the egg in a shallow bowl and lightly beat.

One at a time, bathe each pork chop in the egg, ensuring all sides are covered, then evenly coat each chop in the breadcrumb mixture.

In a large, deep skillet, heat the oil over medium heat. Working in batches, fry the pork chops, flipping, until golden brown, about 3 minutes on each side.

Transfer the pork chops to a large serving plate and serve with lime wedges and chopped cilantro.

Pollo al Curry

Chicken Curry / SERVES 4 TO 6

While curry is not traditional to Mexican cuisine, I grew up eating taquitos with this delicious chicken bathed in my mama's adaptation of curry sauce. What makes her curry distinct is the addition of her not-so-secret ingredient—chicken bouillon. As mentioned in other recipes, my mama often relied on this ingredient to bring flavor to her dishes and it has become a staple in many of my dishes. Instead of adding more salt, I add chicken bouillon. The way to serve this dish is by placing the chicken and sauce on a bed of rice and using tortillas as your tool for eating. Simply place a tortilla on a plate, add a small amount of the Pollo al Curry and rice, top with sour cream, roll it up, and enjoy.

2 teaspoons avocado oil

4 tablespoons unsalted butter

12 chicken breasts, boneless and skinless, cut into 1-inch cubes

2 garlic cloves, minced

¼ teaspoon ground white pepper

2 tablespoons curry powder

1 tablespoon all-purpose flour

Sea salt

1 teaspoon chicken bouillon powder

1 cup dry sherry, plus more as needed

2 tablespoons sour cream

White rice for serving

Chopped cilantro leaves for serving

In a skillet, heat the oil and melt the butter over medium heat. Add the chicken and sear, flipping, until the exterior is golden brown, 2 to 3 minutes on each side. Remove the chicken from the skillet and set aside.

In the same skillet, using the leftover butter and oil, add the garlic, white pepper, curry powder, flour, and a pinch of salt. Sauté over medium heat for 3 minutes.

Dissolve the chicken bouillon powder in ¾ cup of hot water and add to the skillet. Add the sherry and mix well. Return the chicken to the skillet, cover, and cook over low heat, stirring occasionally and adding more sherry as needed if the sauce becomes too thick, for about 25 minutes. The sauce should be a little thinner than a paste, but not super runny. About 5 minutes before serving, stir the sour cream into the sauce. Season with salt. Serve hot with white rice and topped with cilantro.

Pollo al Limón

Chicken with Lime / SERVES 4 TO 6

This is a classic dish that was cooked regularly by Lety, my nanny, who looked after my little sister and me from when Vanessa was born until we moved to the United States. Lety came with us everywhere, including some family vacations. If it had been up to me, Lety would have come to the United States with us and permanently stayed a part of our family. Although there are two thousand miles between us, Lety never stopped being a part of my life, and I still regularly speak with her on Whatsapp. The summer of 2021, when I was able to visit Mexico for the first time in sixteen years, since I immigrated to the United States, I was able to reunite with Lety. The second I saw her, I cried harder than I did when I saw my own auntie, something my auntie remarked on. There are no words that can explain how much Lety means to Team Pons, and how much my life changed after she was no longer physically in it. Embracing her for the first time in years, I realized our heights had changed. She was once the one towering over me, and to my surprise I now could embrace her right beneath my shoulders.

Lety never used a recipe to make this dish, and she never measured anything that went into it. When I was a kid, I loved watching Lety cook, the way she used the molcajete to crush the garlic and onion, creating a trail of scent like someone's perfume that guided you directly into the kitchen. I watched Lety make this dish enough times to be able to recreate it to the best of my memory. When I make this dish, I am reminded of Lety, and all her teachings that helped form me.

TOOLS
Molcajete (mortar and pestle)

6 chicken breasts, boneless
    and skinless
Ground black pepper
2 tablespoons avocado oil
2 tablespoons unsalted butter
1 garlic clove
¼ small white onion
1 lime, zested and juiced
½ teaspoon sea salt
Cooked rice for serving
    (optional)
Lime wedges for serving

Prepare the chicken breasts by trimming off any extra fat, and sprinkle with black pepper.

In a medium stockpot, heat the oil and melt the butter over medium heat. Before the fat begins to smoke, add the chicken and sear, flipping, until the exterior is golden brown, 2 to 3 minutes on each side.

Meanwhile, in a molcajete, crush the garlic and onion into a paste and transfer to a bowl. Add the lime juice, salt, and 1 cup of cold water and mix to combine. Add to the stockpot, cover, and cook over medium-low heat for 15 minutes.

Serve over rice with lime wedges and top with lime zest.

Pollo al Vino Blanco

Chicken in White Wine / SERVES 4 TO 6

This is a dish I often make when I am having people over for dinner. It's become a tradition of sorts to open a bottle of white wine and drink from a glass while making this dish, listening to music, and getting ready to host. The herbed wine marinade is incredibly light and always a crowd pleaser. I get excited to make this dish because to me, there is no better feeling than showing you love someone by making them a meal. This dish pairs well with pretty much anything—I like to serve it with a side of vegetables, or salad. Additionally, it tastes delicious on a bed of garlic mashed potatoes.

6 chicken breasts, boneless and skinless
¼ cup avocado oil
3 large spring onions, bulbs and stems finely sliced
1½ cups dry white wine
¼ teaspoon thyme leaves
¼ teaspoon rosemary needles, roughly chopped
¼ teaspoon dried oregano
¼ teaspoon ground black pepper
Sea salt
Roasted broccoli for serving (optional)
Roasted asparagus for serving (optional)

Prepare the chicken by trimming off any extra fat.

In a soup pot, heat the oil over medium heat. Lightly sear the chicken until golden brown, 2 to 3 minutes on each side. Remove the chicken and set aside. Discard half of the oil from the pot then add the onions and sauté over medium heat for about 5 minutes. Return the chicken to the pot, then add the wine, thyme, rosemary, oregano, and pepper. Season with salt, bring to a boil for 1 minute, then lower the heat to medium-low heat, cover with a lid and simmer for 20 minutes. Serve hot with a side of roasted broccoli or asparagus.

Pollo en Adobo

Chicken in Adobo / SERVES 4 TO 6

The word adobo comes from the Spanish word adobar, which means "to marinate." Many people are familiar with the Filipino dish also called chicken adobo; however, in the Philippines, the meat is marinated in vinegar and soy sauce, while in Mexico we use dried chiles and spices, as well as the addition of potatoes. This dish is smoky with deep flavor. It's one of my favorite dishes to make on a quiet Sunday when there is not a lot going on, and then I can reheat it during the week when I don't feel like cooking. I serve it with rice, which deliciously catches all the sauce, or with a side of corn tortillas to eat it like a taco.

TOOLS
Molcajete (mortar and pestle)

6 chicken breasts, boneless and skinless
4 tablespoons avocado oil
8 dried ancho peppers, seeded
3 garlic cloves
Sea salt
¼ teaspoon ground black pepper
¼ teaspoon ground cinnamon
¼ teaspoon ground cumin
¼ teaspoon dried oregano
2 tablespoons white vinegar
½ pound potatoes, peeled and quartered
2 tablespoons chicken bouillon powder
Cooked white rice for serving

Preheat the oven to 475°F and grease an oven-safe stockpot or Dutch oven with butter.

Prepare the chicken by trimming off any extra fat, and add the chicken to the pot and set aside.

In a skillet, heat 2 tablespoons of the oil over medium heat. Briefly sauté the peppers for about 5 minutes. Transfer to a saucepan, add ½ cup of water, and bring to a boil for 1 minute, then cook over medium heat for 10 minutes, or until the peppers are soft.

Meanwhile, in a molcajete, grind the garlic, ¼ teaspoon of salt, pepper, cinnamon, cumin, oregano, vinegar, and the remaining 2 tablespoons of oil into a paste. Transfer to a large bowl.

In a blender, blend the peppers and liquid until smooth then add to the garlic-herb paste. Pour over the chicken breasts and let marinate for 10 minutes. Add the potatoes. Dissolve the chicken bouillon powder into 2 cups of hot water and add to the stockpot. Cover with aluminum foil and bake for 30 minutes. Serve with a side of white rice.

Bistec con Guacamole

Steak with Guacamole / SERVES 4 TO 6

This plate alone could bankrupt Chipotle restaurants. It's a very traditional way of eating carne, and often made during family or friend gatherings. The word bistec originated from Spanish speakers pronouncing the English words "beef steak." Over time the abbreviated word stuck, and we use it to refer to thin sliced steak, most commonly used for carne asada. I love making this dish in the summer for friends—serving it with a big bowl of guacamole and a side of tortillas—and popping a slice of lime inside a beer bottle.

FOR THE STEAKS
2 tablespoons avocado oil
1 tablespoon Worcestershire sauce
6 sirloin steaks (1½ pounds total)

FOR THE GUACAMOLE
3 ripe Hass avocados
2 firm, medium tomatoes, chopped
½ large white onion, finely chopped
2 garlic cloves, minced
1 jalapeño pepper, seeds removed, and minced
1 bunch cilantro, stems removed and leaves finely chopped
3 tablespoons olive oil
1 lime, juiced
Sea salt
Warm tortillas for serving

Marinate the Steaks
In a small bowl, combine the avocado oil and Worcestershire sauce and mix. Rub all over the steaks and set aside to marinate until you're ready to cook them.

Make the Guacamole
In a medium bowl, mash the avocados until creamy. Add the tomatoes, onion, garlic, jalapeño, cilantro, olive oil, lime juice, and ¼ teaspoon of salt. Taste and adjust salt or lime juice if needed. Mix well. Cover with a lid or plastic wrap, and place the guacamole in the fridge until you're ready to serve.

Cook the Steaks
Heat a large skillet over medium-high heat. Add the steaks. Be careful not to crowd the pan. Sear the steaks, flipping once, until they are golden brown. For medium-rare steaks, sear for 3 to 4 minutes on each side. Serve with the guacamole and a side of warm tortillas.

Pollo con Champiñones

Chicken with Mushrooms / SERVES 4 TO 6

This homey dish was often made by my mama in August when mushrooms were in season. My mama taught me from a young age how to pick ripe produce and eat seasonally—not only for the nutritional value of the food we were consuming but also for the impact that it had on our local community in Mexico. To eat seasonally meant that we were supporting the rancheros living outside of the city who were growing our food. One of those rancheros was my Tio Ricardo, but we called him Richard. Richard isn't my uncle by blood but by the strong bond of friendship. My papa and Richard have been compadres for decades, and I grew up knowing his kids as cousins. Richard and his family owned a farm outside of the city, and during Easter break my family would travel to El Rancho de Richard. We would spend the weekend picking potatoes and corn to bring back to the cabin, and the mamas would take some of the produce to make dinner and place the rest in sacks to bring back home. Richard taught me the importance of caring for the earth—especially the soil that grows our food—and that when you take care of it, in return it takes care of you.

3 tablespoons all-purpose flour

1½ pounds fresh cremini mushrooms

3 tablespoons olive oil

2 medium chicken breasts, boneless and skinless

2 chicken thighs, boneless and skinless

2 skinless chicken drumsticks

½ white onion, finely chopped

2 garlic cloves, minced

3 tablespoons finely chopped parsley leaves

Sea salt

¼ teaspoon ground black pepper

12 ounces light beer (or medium beer)

Cooked rice for serving (optional)

Cooked potatoes for serving (optional)

In a bowl, combine the flour and 3 cups of water and give it a stir. Add the mushrooms and let soak for 15 minutes. Drain the mushrooms and set aside.

Meanwhile, in a large soup pot, heat the oil over medium heat. Prepare the chicken by trimming off any extra fat, then lightly sear the chicken breasts, thighs, and drumsticks in batches, flipping, until it is golden brown, 2 to 3 minutes on each side. Remove the chicken and set aside on a plate.

In the same pot over medium-low heat, sauté the onion, garlic, and parsley in the leftover oil. Return the chicken to the pot and season with salt. Add the black pepper, beer, and mushrooms. Bring to a boil for one minute, then cover the pot with a lid and simmer over medium-low heat until the chicken is fully cooked, about 15 minutes. Season with salt as needed.

Serve with a side of rice or potatoes.

Albondigas Borrachas

Drunken Meatballs / SERVES 4 TO 6

I grew up eating these albondigas borrachas as a weekend meal, served with rice and potatoes, as I instruct here. But once I started living on my own and began writing this book, I experimented with serving these as appetizers and they were a hit! If you'd like to go that route, you can double the batch and make the meatballs a lot smaller, place a toothpick inside each of them, and serve them at your next gathering. Don't worry, you can thank me later.

1 pound ground pork
1 pound ground beef
1 garlic clove, minced
2 large eggs, lightly beaten
¼ teaspoon ground
    black pepper
3 tablespoons panko
    breadcrumbs
¼ teaspoon Italian seasoning
Sea salt
3 tablespoons all-purpose
    flour
4 tablespoons avocado oil
3 tablespoons finely
    chopped onion
2 tablespoons finely
    chopped parsley leaves
2 medium tomatoes, finely
    chopped
12 ounces light beer
Mashed potatoes for serving
    (optional)
Cooked rice for serving
    (optional)

In a large bowl, mix the pork, beef, garlic, eggs, pepper, breadcrumbs, Italian seasoning, and a generous pinch of salt. With your hands, make 1½-inch meatballs.

In a shallow bowl or plate, add the flour. Roll the meatballs in the flour.

In a skillet, heat 3 tablespoons of the oil over medium heat. Add the meatballs and sear on all sides until golden brown. Remove the skillet from the heat and set the meatballs aside on a plate.

In a soup pot, heat the remaining 1 tablespoon of oil over medium heat. Sauté the onions, parsley, and tomatoes. Add the beer, ¼ cup of cold water, and the meatballs. Season with salt as needed. Cover and cook for 15 minutes. Serve hot with a side of mashed potatoes or rice.

Carne en Salsa Verde con Papas

Pork in Green Sauce with Potatoes / SERVES 4 TO 6

El Día del Padre in my household is always celebrated with a big plate of this Carne en Salsa Verde con Papas. My dad rarely likes to enchilarse (purposely eat spicy food to feel a burn), so he has always loved when my mama cooks dishes like this, which have all the flavor but very mild spiciness. I grew up to really love this dish, specially rolled up in a tortilla with a little bit of crema to make the salsa creamier. The green color comes from the tomatillos, but unlike their name suggests, tomatillos are not "little tomatoes," or tomatoes at all, for that matter. Think of them rather as a cousin of the tomato. While tomatillos can turn yellow, red, or even purple with full maturity, they are only eaten unripe in Mexican dishes. When shopping for tomatillos look for ones that have dry and papery husks, avoiding those that feel moist, look shriveled, or feel damp. If buying tomatillos ahead of time, store them in a cool dry place and never place them inside the fridge.

1 pound boneless pork loin, cut into 1-inch cubes
Sea salt and ground black pepper
½ teaspoon garlic powder
1 tablespoon olive oil
2 cups husked, rinsed, and halved tomatillos
¼ medium white onion
1 garlic clove, minced
2 jalapeño peppers, seeded
2 tablespoons chicken bouillon powder
2 cups halved baby potatoes
Cooked rice for serving
Warm tortillas for serving

Season the pork loin with salt, pepper, and garlic powder.

In a deep, medium skillet, heat the oil over medium heat. Sear the pork, flipping, until browned, 2 to 3 minutes on each side. Do not cook the pork all the way through. Remove the pork from the pan and set aside.

In a blender, combine the tomatillos, onion, garlic, jalapeños, chicken bouillon powder, and 4 cups of cold water. Blend well.

In the same skillet, add the sauce, bring to a simmer over medium heat for 2 minutes. Add the pork and baby potatoes and bring to a boil over medium-high heat. Reduce the heat to low, cover, and simmer until the potatoes are soft, about 30 minutes. Serve with a side of rice and warm tortillas.

Carne de Puerco con Rajas en Salsa de Tomate

Pork Chops in Spicy Tomato and Poblano Sauce / SERVES 4 TO 6

This meat is a year-round family favorite in my home. Tender pork chops in a semi-spicy tomato sauce are topped with silky poblano strips. This dish is traditionally served alongside Torta de Elote (page 107), where the sweetness of the corn cake balances out the savoriness of this pork dish. If you prefer to serve this without the corn cake, you can substitute rice and a side of tortillas instead. It's important to add the rajas as your last step; that way, they don't lose too much of their texture and become too soft in the stew.

FOR THE SAUCE
3 medium poblano peppers
1 medium jalapeño pepper
7 medium Roma tomatoes
1 tablespoon chicken bouillon powder
1 teaspoon fresh oregano leaves, chopped
1 (8-ounce) can tomato sauce

FOR THE PORK
4 pounds boneless pork chops, cut into 1-inch cubes
1 tablespoon garlic salt
1 tablespoon ground black pepper
2 tablespoons avocado oil
2 large white onions, thinly sliced
2 garlic cloves, minced

TOPPINGS
Queso fresco
Sour cream

Make the Sauce
Heat a medium, dry skillet over medium-high heat, then add the poblano peppers and sear, turning, until brown and blistered all over. Once the poblanos are blistered, place them in an airtight container or seal them in a plastic bag to sweat for about 10 minutes. This will help remove the outer skin.

Heat a large, dry skillet over medium-high heat, then add the jalapeño and whole tomatoes and sear, turning, until brown and blistered all over. Remove the stems from the jalapeño then cut in half and remove the veins and seeds; if you like your sauce on the spicier end, keep the seeds of the jalapeño. Place in a blender, along with the tomatoes, chicken bouillon powder, and blend until smooth. Set aside.

Make the Pork
In a large bowl, season the cubed pork with garlic salt and pepper and toss until all pieces are evenly coated.

In the same large skillet used to sear the peppers and tomatoes, heat the avocado oil over medium-high heat. Working in batches as needed to avoid crowding the meat, add the pork and sear, flipping, for 1 to 2 minutes until browned. Add the onion and garlic and cook until they become fragrant, about 3 minutes. Add the blended jalapeño-tomato sauce, followed by the can of tomato sauce, and gently mix until fully incorporated. Reduce the heat to medium, cover, and simmer for 30 minutes.

Meanwhile, remove the poblano peppers from their container or plastic bag and under gentle cold running water, massage the peppers with your fingers to loosen up the outer skin, and remove as much of it as possible. Using a knife, slice the poblanos in half to remove the inner veins and seeds, then slice the peppers lengthwise to create ½-inch wide strips. These are your "rajas."

Add the rajas and oregano to the pork, cover, and simmer over medium-low heat for 5 more minutes or until ready to serve. Serve pork warm with a slice of Torta de Elote (page 107), queso fresco, and sour cream.

Lomo en Salsa de Ciruela

Pork Loin in Prune Sauce / SERVES 4 TO 6

This meal was traditionally made by my Titita Tere every Christmas, in place of the baked ham many people in the United States eat. The marinade is rich and sweet, and the prunes and almonds add texture to each bite. Navidad was a very big deal in my family, and we always spent it at Titita's house. Gifts were opened only after dinner—an event that as a kid felt like it lasted an eternity. Mainly because the parents lingered sobremesa, sipping on rompope, Mexico's version of spiked eggnog, and eating galletitas (cookies). Although I didn't realize it then, this dish was a gift, a way for Titita to tell us all how much she loved us, that we were valued. Titita Tere's Alzheimer's has been one of the most devastating events in our family, and Navidad has not been the same since she's been unable to look after herself. Being able to make this dish now, in my own home, is a way that I can honor her love and resilience.

4 tablespoons olive oil

½ cup chopped bacon

¾ medium white onion, chopped

4 garlic cloves, minced

2 cups cola

3 tablespoons chicken bouillon powder

3 tablespoons Maggi sauce

2 tablespoons Worcestershire sauce

2 tablespoons brown sugar

½ cup pitted dried prunes

6 pork loin chops

Sea salt and ground black pepper

1 tablespoon slivered almonds

Cooked white rice for serving (optional)

Mashed potatoes for serving (optional)

In a large skillet, heat 2 tablespoons of the oil over medium-high heat. Add the bacon and cook. Before the bacon becomes crispy, add the onion and garlic. Reduce the heat to medium and sauté until the onion is translucent, about 3 minutes. Add the cola, chicken bouillon powder, Maggi sauce, Worcestershire sauce, brown sugar, and prunes. Mix well then remove from the heat and set aside.

In a separate skillet, heat the remaining 2 tablespoons of oil over medium heat. Generously season the pork with salt and pepper. Add to the pan and sear, flipping, until both sides begin to brown but the meat is not cooked all the way through. Remove from the heat.

Set the skillet with the sauce over medium-high heat and bring to a boil. Add the pork and almonds, reduce the heat to medium, and cook until the sauce reduces, about 20 minutes.

Serve the pork topped with the prune sauce and with a side of white rice or mashed potatoes.

Mariscos

Bacalao a la Vizcaina

Spanish Salt Cod Stew / SERVES 4 TO 6

While my mama's side of the family traditionally ate Lomo en Salsa de Ciruela (page 136) for Navidad, my papa grew up eating this Spanish salted cod stew in his home. Each year since we moved to the United States my mama takes turns making her childhood favorite or my papa's. It's so hard to choose my favorite since they are entirely different and both come loaded with memories of being surrounded by my cousins during the holidays. Maybe because I grew up inland in Mexico, I have always had a soft spot for fish (shh, don't let my mama know). When I was younger, I only knew bacalao to come in a small wooden box, before being rinsed and left to soak for hours, sometimes even a full day. When I traveled to Portugal in 2019, I saw fish markets with bacalao everywhere—beautiful long sheets of fish, salted and ready to be made into delicious stew. My mama makes this dish on the watery side, so we can eat it almost like soup, but you can make it a thicker stew and eat it with rice. Whatever your preference, the key is in allowing the fish enough time to rehydrate.

1½ pounds salt cod (bacalao)

2 pounds Roma tomatoes

1 pound roasting potatoes, peeled and quartered

¼ cup olive oil

1 large white onion, thinly sliced

4 garlic cloves, minced

¾ cup pitted and halved green olives

⅓ cup raisins

2 tablespoons capers

2 cups sliced roasted red bell peppers (from a jar)

6 pickled Güero peppers (yellow chile peppers)

1 bunch parsley, stems removed and leaves chopped (about 1 cup)

1½ teaspoons dried oregano

Sea salt and ground black pepper

Cooked rice for serving

Dinner rolls for serving

Gently rinse the salt cod 3 times under cold running water until the water runs clear. Soak the salt cod in a container of cold water in the fridge for at least 8 hours (or overnight) to rehydrate the fish and remove excess salt.

Rinse the salt cod and set aside.

In a large soup pot, combine the salt cod and 5 cups of cold water. Bring to a boil for 1 minute, then simmer over medium heat for 7 minutes. Drain the salt cod, reserving ½ cup of the cooking liquid. Set aside.

In a large skillet or hot griddle, roast the tomatoes whole over medium-high heat for about 10 minutes until they begin to brown and the skins become soft and cracked.

Meanwhile, shred the salt cod using two forks and set aside.

In a blender, blend the roasted tomatoes until smooth. Using a strainer, strain the blended tomatoes into a bowl and set aside.

In a large soup pot, combine the potatoes and enough water to cover and bring to a boil over medium-high heat. Continue boiling the potatoes until tender enough to pierce with a butter knife, about 30 minutes. Drain the potatoes and set aside.

In a large skillet, heat the oil over medium-high heat. Add the onion and cook until translucent, about 4 minutes. Reduce the heat to medium, add the garlic, and cook for 3 minutes. Add the roasted tomato sauce and bring to a boil for 1 minute, then lower the heat back to medium and simmer for 5 to 7 minutes.

Add the shredded salt cod and simmer over medium heat for 5 minutes. Add the olives, raisins, and capers, stir gently with a wooden spoon, and simmer for another 5 minutes. Add the potatoes, red bell peppers, Güero peppers, parsley, and oregano. Taste and season with salt as needed. Continue to simmer until the sauce has reduced. Serve hot with a side of rice and dinner rolls.

Conchitas de Pescado

Fish Gratin in Scallop Shells / MAKES 8 TO 12 SHELLS

Buttery fish, blanketed in cheese and baked to a golden crisp—what's not to love about that? These conchitas de pescado make a delightful appetizer, and the presentation of the fish in the scallop shells is always a conversation starter. It's important when looking for scallop shells that you purchase natural ones that are good for baking. Replica shells made of unnatural ingredients can burn, melt, or give your dish an unexpected taste. Sometimes I can find them at fish markets by asking the fishmonger if they have any discarded scallop shells. I like to garnish the baked shells with chopped chives or green onion before serving them for a pop of color.

TOOLS
12 large baking scallop shells

**½ pound fresh tilapia
   (or grouper)**
1 lime, juiced
Sea salt
4 tablespoons unsalted butter
**2 tablespoons all-purpose
   flour**
½ cup whole milk
**½ cup shredded Manchego
   cheese**

Preheat the oven to 475°F and line a sheet pan with aluminum foil.

Rinse the tilapia under cold running water, then drizzle with a few drops of lime juice.

In a large skillet, add the tilapia, a pinch of salt, and 1 cup of water. Cover and cook over low heat for 8 minutes. Remove the tilapia and pat dry with paper towels. Shred in a bowl using two forks and set aside.

In a medium saucepan, melt the butter over medium heat, then add the flour. Gently whisk the flour into the butter until the roux begins to turn golden brown. Add the milk, 1 tablespoon at a time, whisking until combined. Remove from the heat, add half of the cheese, and whisk until the sauce is smooth. Add the shredded fish and gently mix into the sauce.

Divide the fish and sauce evenly among the scallop shells and place on the sheet pan. Top each portion with the rest of the cheese. Bake for 5 to 10 minutes, or until the cheese is melted and golden. Serve hot.

Cebiche

SERVES 4 TO 6

Ceviche or cebiche? The spelling depends only on what zone in Mexico you are eating this dish. Because I grew up knowing it as cebiche I decided to keep this spelling instead of ceviche, which is more commonly known in the United States. Like the variation in spelling, this dish has many modifications of ingredients depending on the region and who is making it. A lot of my mama's recipes have a strong Spanish influence, which you can see in the addition of olives to many of her recipes, including this one. I like cutting my fish into cubes instead of strips. The cubes must be bite-sized—not too small and not too big—as traditionally, cebiche is served in a bowl and scooped up with tortilla chips to eat.

½ **pound fresh halibut fillet (or swordfish)**
1 **lime, juiced**
1 **teaspoon sea salt**
4 **medium tomatoes**
½ **medium white onion, chopped**
1 **garlic clove, minced**
1 **bunch cilantro leaves, chopped**
10 **green olives, pitted and halved**
2 **large jalapeño peppers, seeded and coarsely chopped**
1 **medium Hass avocado, cubed**
¼ **cup olive oil**
2 **teaspoons white wine vinegar**

Rinse the halibut under cold running water and pat dry. Chop into ½-inch cubes.

In a salad bowl, bathe the halibut in the lime juice, tossing so it doesn't "cook" unevenly. Season with salt and cover the bowl with plastic wrap. Place the bowl in the fridge for 1 hour.

In a medium saucepan, combine the tomatoes and enough water to cover them. Bring to a boil over medium-high heat and cook until the skins begin to split, about 1 minute. Drain and rinse the tomatoes under cold running water. Remove the skins with a paper towel. Chop the tomatoes into small cubes and set aside.

Remove the halibut from the fridge, add the tomatoes, then add the onion, garlic, cilantro, olives, peppers, avocado, olive oil, and vinegar. Mix gently. Taste and season with salt as needed. Serve with crackers or tortilla chips.

Deditos de Pescado

Fish Fingers / SERVES 3 TO 4

I never grew up eating chicken nuggets for a meal at home, or any sort of take-out, for that matter. The only exception was once in a blue moon when my parents would take my sister and me to the local mall, where there was a McDonald's that had a playground. In between pretending to drown in the ball pen and sliding down a snake-shaped tunnel, I took bites of those golden miniature pillows. And although I preferred chicken nuggets to my sister's burger, which could've passed for a Frisbee, nothing compared to when my mama would have fresh deditos de pescado ready after school. When American kids are picky with dinner or parents are in a rush, chicken nuggets come to the rescue, but in my home, it was these golden, flaky fish fingers. Once you eat one, you almost can't stop. They are addictively crunchy and easy to make. Say hello to your new favorite snack and goodbye to the freezer-burned nuggets.

3 pounds fresh sea bass
(or grouper)
½ lime, juiced
2 large eggs
2 cups panko breadcrumbs
1 teaspoon sea salt, plus more
to taste
1 teaspoon ground black
pepper, plus more to taste
½ cup avocado oil
Ketchup for serving (optional)
Hot sauce for serving
(optional)
Tartar sauce for serving
(optional)

Using a sharp knife, slice the sea bass into strips the length and width of your index finger. Place the strips in a bowl, add the lime juice, and mix. Cover the bowl with plastic wrap and let the sea bass rest in the fridge for 10 minutes.

In a bowl, beat the eggs until the whites and yolks are fully incorporated. In a shallow plate or tray, mix the panko, salt, and pepper.

One at a time, dip each fish strip into the eggs, then roll in the panko mixture, tapping down, so the whole surface is evenly covered. Set aside.

In a skillet, heat the oil over medium-high heat. Fry 3 strips of fish at a time until golden brown, 3 to 5 minutes on each side. Be careful not to burn the panko coating. Set the finished fish fingers on a baking rack lined with paper towels to remove any excess oil. Serve hot with ketchup, hot sauce, or tartar sauce.

Pescado en Salsa Verde

Fish in Green Sauce / SERVES 4 TO 6

There is a lot of conversation about where this fish in green sauce originated. Some say that it started in the Basque Country of Spain and became adopted by Central and South America. I have eaten Cuban-style pescado en salsa verde—which gets its color from parsley and is made with white wine—however, in my recipe, tomatillos, cilantro, and green chiles are what give the sauce its beautiful green color, while also honoring many ingredients native to Mexico. This dish is mildly spicy and can be made spicier by adding thin slices of jalapeño as garnish.

2 cups husked and rinsed
    tomatillos
¼ medium white onion
1 garlic clove
1 bunch cilantro, stems
    removed and leaves
    coarsely chopped
4 Mexican pepper leaves
    (or Thai basil)
5 serrano peppers
4 tablespoons olive oil
3 pounds (6 fillets) fresh
    sea bass (or grouper)
2 tablespoons unsalted butter
Sea salt
Cooked white rice for serving
    (optional)

Preheat the oven to 400°F. Grease a 9x13-inch glass baking dish with butter.

In a large soup pot, combine the tomatillos, onion, garlic, cilantro, pepper leaves, serrano peppers, and 1 cup of water. Bring to a boil for 1 minute, reduce heat to medium and simmer for 2 to 5 minutes. Transfer to a blender and blend well.

In a skillet, heat the oil over medium-high heat. Add the blended sauce and cook for 3 minutes.

Add the sea bass to the buttered baking dish, then bathe the fillets in the sauce. Cover the baking dish with aluminum foil and bake for 12 to 15 minutes. Do not cook for more than 15 minutes, or the fish will be overcooked.

Top the sea bass with more sauce and serve with a side of white rice.

Cebiche de Camarón

Shrimp Cebiche / SERVES 4 TO 6

My earliest memory of this dish coincides with the first time I ate a fresh clam. It was a few days before the year 2000 and my family decided to go to Puerto Vallarta to celebrate the turn of the decade. We were at the beach and my parents ordered cebiche de camarón, which was served in a giant coupe glass overflowing with avocado slices and shrimp. It was love at first bite. Later on that trip, sitting just inches away from the water's reach, my sister and I began to dig. I was trying to dig deep enough and wide enough to bury my lower body when suddenly I found a beautiful clam. I placed it in my bucket with salty water and sand before running up to my papa. I lifted the clam and proudly handed it over to him. To my shock, he took out his Swiss army knife, popped my little friend open, squeezed lime inside its walls, and handed it back to me with the words, "try it." I pressed the shell up to my lips before slurping up a salty and silky gummy. Once again, it was love at first bite. For the rest of the trip, I wanted nothing more than to order cebiche de camarón and spend hours at the beach, digging for more clams.

3 large firm tomatoes

½ large white onion, finely chopped

½ medium Hass avocado, cubed

10 green olives, pitted and halved

¾ pound shrimp, peeled and deveined

5 limes, juiced

5 tablespoons olive oil

Sea salt and ground black pepper

¼ cup finely chopped cilantro leaves

Tostadas (or salted crackers) for serving

In a medium saucepan, combine the tomatoes and enough water to cover them. Bring to a boil and cook until the skins begin to split, about 1 minute. Drain and rinse the tomatoes under cold running water. Remove the skins with a paper towel then chop.

In a large bowl, combine the tomatoes, onion, avocado, and olives. Carefully mix in the shrimp, lime juice, and olive oil. Season with salt and black pepper. Cover with plastic wrap, and place the cebiche in the fridge until chilled, 30 minutes to 1 hour.

Serve in large cups topped with cilantro and enjoy with tostadas or salted crackers.

Queso Cottage con Sardinas

Cottage Cheese with Sardines / SERVES 2 TO 4

Sardines with cheese in the morning might sound strange to most people who grew up believing that a bowl of cereal, a piece of white toast, and a glass of orange juice are what make up a balanced breakfast. But in my opinion, nothing is more fueling than this protein- and omega-3-rich breakfast. In Mexico, cottage cheese is often served for breakfast, either on toast or as a topping for fruit instead of yogurt. When I moved away for college, I rarely had time to cook anything complicated for breakfast or sometimes even lunch, and this dish saved me through many busy days in the sewing lab while I was trying to obtain my fashion degree (a story for another time). It's simple enough to make in the morning or enjoy as an afternoon snack in between meals.

1 cup cottage cheese

2 teaspoons soy sauce

6 sardines in oil, spines removed

2 bunches large spring onions

6 large leaf lettuce leaves

4 toasted sourdough bread slices (or salted crackers) for serving

In a bowl, combine the cottage cheese and soy sauce. Carefully add the sardines.

Thinly slice the spring onions. Separate the onion bulb slices from the stem slices. Add the bulb slices to the cottage cheese mixture and gently mix.

Place 2 tablespoons of the sardine mixture in the center of each lettuce leaf.

Top with remaining sliced onion stems and serve with toast or salted crackers.

Pescado en Salsa de Hierbabuena

Fish in Mint Sauce / SERVES 4 TO 6

This is one of my favorite dishes to make during the summer months. Besides being incredibly delicious, mint contains menthol, an organic compound that triggers cold receptors in our skin and mouth resulting in a cooling sensation that is perfect for hot days. I like serving it the Spanish way, with a side of baked potatoes; however, if you are looking for something lighter, a fresh side salad with cucumber (another cooling ingredient) goes perfectly with this fish. Serve with a glass of chilled white wine and you have an ideal meal.

TOOLS
Cheesecloth
Twine

3 pounds (6 fillets) large sea bass (or halibut)
1 garlic clove
½ leek
1 dried bay leaf
1½ teaspoons sea salt, divided
1 cup finely chopped mint leaves
½-inch knob fresh ginger, peeled and minced
1 teaspoon fresh lime juice
¼ cup white vinegar
1 teaspoon granulated sugar
Steamed or baked potatoes for serving

Rinse the sea bass under cold running water and pat dry. Wrap a fillet in cheesecloth and make a parcel by tying both ends using twine. Repeat with each fillet for a total of 6 parcels.

In a large soup pot, bring 2 cups of water to a boil over high heat. Add the garlic, leek, bay leaf, and 1 teaspoon of salt. Add the sea bass parcels and reduce the heat to medium-low until you have a gentle boil. Cover the pot and cook for 35 to 40 minutes, or until the fish is tender enough to easily shred with a fork. Turn off the heat but leave the pot on the heat source while you prepare the salsa.

In a bowl, combine the mint, ginger, lime juice, vinegar and sugar, and ½ teaspoon salt. Mix well.

Carefully remove the sea bass from the pot, and gently open each parcel without breaking the fillets. Transfer the sea bass to a serving plate. Bathe in the mint sauce and serve with steamed or baked potatoes.

Pulpos en su Tinta

Octopus in Ink / SERVES 4 TO 6

Cooking octopus can be quite a challenge if you have never done it before. The meat of an octopus is essentially one big muscle that can be tough if not properly tenderized. My solution to this problem is a pressure cooker, a tool that my mama could not live without—and now following in her steps, I can't either. Pressure-cooking octopus allows you to reduce the time it would take to simmer and braise the octopus to a tender softness. Shop for a fresh octopus, and if possible, ask the fishmonger to clean and behead the octopus for you, reserving the ink. If you are only able to find frozen octopus, don't worry. The freezing process can be to your benefit because it tenderizes the meat and the octopus will already be cleaned. Allow the meat to fully thaw before making this dish and you'll be good to go.

1½ **pounds octopus, plus reserved ink (see note above)**
2 **large tomatoes, chopped**
1 **medium white onion, chopped**
3 **garlic cloves**
1 **tablespoon olive oil**
24 **ounces light beer**
1½ **teaspoons sea salt**
10 **green olives, pitted and halved**
10 **capers, drained**
Cooked white rice for serving

Rinse the octopus under cold running water. Chop into small, bite-sized cubes. Set aside.

In a blender, combine the tomatoes, onion, and garlic. Blend well.

In a large pressure cooker, heat the olive oil over medium heat. Add the blended tomato sauce. Fry the sauce until the oil begins to separate. Add the octopus, beer, and salt and continue cooking over medium heat. Cover the pot and once the steam starts to escape, seal the valve. When the pot begins to whistle, set a timer for 1 hour.

After 1 hour, carefully cool the pot under cold running water. Once the pot is cool enough to release the valve, uncover the lid. Add the reserved octopus ink, olives, and capers. Leave the octopus to season in the ink until the sauce starts to thicken, 6 to 8 minutes. Serve immediately with white rice.

Aguachile

Shrimp with Green Salsa / SERVES 2 TO 4

Aguachile is a road map to the history of Mexican culture. Before the Spanish conquest in the sixteenth century, Indigenous communities lived in the precipitous hills that make up modern-day Sinaloa's eastern border. The Indigenous people would dry meat and carry it from those rugged hills down to the Pacific coast, where they would trade the meat for salt with the civilizations that were established there.

In a container similar to a molcajete, salt would be mixed with a berry-sized chile called chiltepín. Although small in size, chiltepín is packed with heat unlike any other pepper in Mexico. Together, the salt and chiltepín would be ground with the addition of water that traveled eleven rivers and countless streams across Sinaloa's hills before joining the seafood-rich lagoons of the Pacific coast. This mixture is a kind of pre-Hispanic salsa and got its name for the two primary ingredients used: agua (water) and chile (pepper), hence the name aguachile.

Unfortunately, the production of chiltepín has declined since the nineteenth century, when dictator Porfirio Díaz sold off massive amounts of Indigenous land to foreign investors for industrialized farming. Throughout the twentieth century, there was no effort to control deforestation, which has eliminated the majority of the wild chiltepín habitat. Due to this, chiltepín can mostly be found only in the "golden triangle" that is formed by the borders of Sinaloa, Durango, and Chihuahua. If you wanted to get your hands on some fresh chiltepín, you would need access to someone who has contacts in that area. Not an easy task.

This lack of access to chiltepín has resulted in adaptations of aguachile over the years. Today, most aguachile dishes are made with cousins of chiltepín such as serrano peppers and jalapeños. There is no trace of when shrimp began to appear as part of this dish. Some suspect it was Japanese migrant influence, but we have no record of this. What is important, however, is that we continue to honor its Indigenous history.

When making this dish, it is best practice to use sustainably sourced shrimp. Any shrimp will do, but if you want the real deal, blue shrimp is what is traditionally used. And unlike ceviche, which utilizes the acidity of lime to cook the shrimp, this dish is traditionally served with semi-raw shrimp, which gives it a chewy and soft texture.

RECIPE CONTINUES ⟶

Aguachile / Shrimp with Green Salsa

FOR THE SHRIMP
1 pound raw shrimp,
    peeled and deveined
    (tails optional)
2 large limes
¼ teaspoon sea salt

FOR THE RED ONION
¼ red onion, thinly sliced
2 teaspoons white vinegar
¼ teaspoon sea salt

FOR THE SALSA
2 serrano peppers
1 jalapeño pepper
1 garlic clove
4 large limes
1 cup chopped cilantro
    (with some stems)
Sea salt and ground black
    pepper
½ cup round cucumber slices

FOR SERVING
Tostadas
Cucumber slices
Avocado slices
Lime wedges
Cilantro

Make the Shrimp

Place the shrimp in a shallow bowl or on plate, making sure the shrimp do not overlap. Squeeze the juice from the 2 limes over the shrimp. This will cause the shrimp to "cook." Sprinkle with the salt, cover with plastic wrap, and place in the fridge for 20 minutes, flipping the shrimp halfway through.

Make the Red Onion

In a medium bowl, cover the onions with the white vinegar and salt. Add just enough water to submerge the onions. Put aside for 5 to 10 minutes while you make the salsa.

Make the Salsa

Halve the peppers lengthwise and remove their seeds (do this only if you like a less spicy salsa; I like mine spicy, so I keep all the seeds). Cut off and discard the tops of the peppers, then add the peppers to a blender or food processor. Add the garlic, the juice from the 4 limes, and the cilantro leaves and stems. Season with salt and pepper and blend until smooth.

Assemble the Aguachile

Drain the onions from their liquid, then add the onions to the salsa. Pour the salsa over the shrimp and toss to coat every shrimp. Add sliced cucumber, if using, then cover with plastic wrap and refrigerate for 30 minutes to 4 hours before serving. This dish is best cold!

To serve, place a small amount of aguachile on a tostada topped with cucumber slices, avocado slices, an extra squeeze of lime (I like mine very citrusy), and more cilantro for garnish. Add extra salt as needed, but only after trying it on a tostada first!

Pescado a la Veracruzana

Veracruz-Style Fish / SERVES 4 TO 6

Pescado a la Veracruzana is Veracruz's state dish, and for good reason. This dish is delicious and comes together in about thirty minutes, making it a perfect weeknight dinner. Veracruz is one of Mexico's oldest and largest ports, and many of the dishes that come from there—especially the seafood dishes—are loaded with Spanish and European influences, reflected in the cooking methods as well as the ingredients. Olives and capers, both found in this dish, originally traveled overseas to Mexico by boat and gradually became a part of Mexican cuisine. Traditionally this dish is made with red snapper, but as that can be harder to come by, I adapted the recipe to use black sea bass or grouper in its place.

3 pounds (6 fillets) fresh black sea bass (or grouper)

1 lime, juiced

3 tablespoons olive oil

2 green bell peppers, sliced into strips

¾ medium white onion, sliced into rounds

1 garlic clove, minced

5 large tomatoes

6 green olives, pitted and halved

5 capers, halved

1 tablespoon chicken bouillon powder

4 pickled Mexican hot peppers (or pickled jalapeño peppers), sliced

Rinse the sea bass under cold running water, then drizzle with a few drops of lime juice. Set aside on a plate.

In a large skillet, heat the oil over medium heat. Add the bell peppers, onion, and garlic. Sauté until the onion becomes translucent, about 5 minutes.

Meanwhile, in a medium soup pot, combine the tomatoes and enough water to cover and bring to a boil over medium-high heat. Cook the tomatoes until the skins begin to split, about 1 minute. Drain and rinse the tomatoes under cold running water. Remove the skins with a paper towel. Core and cube the tomatoes. Add the tomatoes, along with the olives, capers, and chicken bouillon powder to the onion mixture. Reduce the heat to medium-low, cover, and simmer for 5 to 8 minutes. Add the sea bass and bathe it in the sauce. Cover and cook over low heat for about 15 minutes, or until the fish is opaque and flaky. Serve immediately, topped with the sliced pickled peppers.

Postres

Arroz con Leche

Rice Pudding / SERVES 4 TO 6

On most occasions, if we were asked what we wanted for dessert, my little sister Vanessa would answer arroz con leche. This dessert has traveled the world. It first originated in Muslim culture before it was adapted by Spain and later brought to Central and South America. In Mexico, we believe arroz con leche heals the soul and brightens your day. While it is traditionally eaten as dessert, this makes a great breakfast. If you're vegan or avoiding dairy, you can substitute the condensed and evaporated milk for condensed coconut or oat milk and evaporated coconut or oat milk. Arroz con leche can be enjoyed warm or cold, but traditionally in Mexico we eat it after it's been chilled.

2 cinnamon sticks

3 to 5 whole cloves

¼ teaspoon sea salt

¾ cup long-grain white rice

¾ cup evaporated milk

½ cup sweetened condensed milk

1 cup dark raisins

1 tablespoon ground cinnamon, for topping

In a medium saucepan, combine the cinnamon sticks, cloves, salt, and 4 cups of water and bring to a boil. Continue boiling for 5 minutes. Remove from the heat, cover, and steep for 1 hour.

Using a strainer, strain the liquid and discard the cinnamon sticks and cloves. Return the liquid to the pan. Add the rice and bring to a boil over medium heat for 1 minute, reduce heat to medium-high, and cook for 10 minutes. Add the evaporated milk and condensed milk. Continue to cook over medium heat for 15 minutes. Stir in the raisins and cook for another 5 minutes.

Ladle the rice pudding into small bowls and sprinkle cinnamon on top. Cover and refrigerate for at least 2 hours (or overnight). Serve chilled.

Nieve de Limón

Lime Sorbet / SERVES 4 TO 6

Every day after school, kids would spill into a gated courtyard that was shared by all the grades, where we would wait for our parents to pick us up. Right outside the gates, vendors parked their cars and sold all sorts of goods from their trunks—there was the empanadas lady, the tamales lady, a man selling balloons. But the only vendor allowed inside the courtyard was Chávez, the local ice-cream man. Chávez, whose first name I never learned, was a sweet soul not much taller than the metal icebox filled with gallon buckets of different flavors of ice-cream that he would wheel around the neighborhood. For two pesos I could get a scoop of any flavor in a cup, but nieve de limón was my favorite. I modified this childhood treat by creating a mint sauce that pairs beautifully with the acidity of the lime. I guarantee, on any hot summer day, that this dessert will have you grinning.

1 large bunch mint, stems
    removed
1 cup granulated sugar
2 pints lime sorbet

In a blender, combine the mint, sugar, and ½ cup of water. Blend well.

In a saucepan, bring the mint mixture to a boil over medium-high heat for 1 minute, lower to medium heat and cook while stirring for 4 minutes. Remove from the heat, transfer to a metal bowl, and chill in the freezer for 15 minutes.

Using a large ice cream scoop, scoop the sorbet into 4 to 6 serving cups. Top each cup with the mint sauce. Store any leftover sauce in the freezer or fridge.

Duraznos al Horno

Baked Peaches / SERVES 4 TO 6

Peaches arrived in Mexico during the Spanish conquest of the 1500s; however, peach production was limited to the gardens of nobility. It wasn't until centuries later, in 1927, when peaches began to be grown for public consumption and commerce. Mexico currently produces over 164,000 tons of peaches per year, most of them exported into the United States for consumption. With time, Mexico began to adopt peaches into our cuisine, resulting in delicious desserts, including carlotta de durazno, gelatinas de durazno, and pastel de tres leches con durazno. But my favorite approach to this fruit has always been: keep it simple. Buttery baked peaches with a cloud of whipped cream or vanilla ice cream are sure to make you feel like royalty.

12 ripe peaches, pitted and halved
½ cup granulated sugar
1 cup very cold whipping cream
4 teaspoons confectioners' sugar

Preheat the oven to 300°F. Grease a glass 9x13-inch baking dish with butter.

Arrange the peaches, cut-sides up in the dish, leaving 1 inch of space between them. Sprinkle the granulated sugar over the peaches and bake for 20 minutes.

Meanwhile, in a stand mixer, beat the very cold whipping cream on medium-high until it begins to thicken. Add the confectioners' sugar and beat for about 2 more minutes until the whipped cream is soft and fluffy. You are looking for medium peaks. Be careful not to overwhip. Remove the peaches from the oven and serve warm with the whipped cream.

Plátanos con Crema

Bananas in Cream / SERVES 4 TO 6

This dessert or snack was my favorite thing to have for merienda. Merienda in Mexico is considered an afternoon or evening snack, usually eaten around seven to nine o'clock. With hair dripping from a shower and my comfiest pajamas on, I would cuddle up in my parents' bedroom, with a bowl of plátanos con crema while my sister and I watched TV before bedtime. There is really nothing fancy about this dessert—it's just creamy and delicious. The important ingredient is the sour cream, which has to be a Mexican-style crema. Mexican sour cream is richer and a bit more sour in flavor than American sour cream, which helps balance out the sweetness of the bananas and additional sugar. Sprinkle with cinnamon, add granola for a crunchier bite if you'd like, and enjoy by the spoonful.

1 cup Mexican crema or sour cream

2 tablespoons granulated sugar

⅛ teaspoon ground cinnamon, plus more for serving

5 ripe bananas, peeled and thickly sliced (no brown spots)

Granola for topping (optional)

In a medium bowl, combine the sour cream, sugar, and cinnamon and mix together. Fold the bananas into the cream mixture. Serve with a sprinkle of cinnamon and granola.

Trufas de Chocolate

Chocolate Truffles / **MAKES ABOUT 8 TRUFFLES**

Growing up, I attended school at a Catholic institute, where I learned to make these chocolate truffles from the nuns who lived in the convent that was a part of my school. La Madre Maria de Lourdes was my First Communion mentor, and she taught my third-grade class how to make these trufas de chocolate by hand so we could gift them to our mamas for Día de la Madre. I loved the process of making these little gestures of love, and to this day, I like to make a batch of them every year on Mother's Day. They are also a great "cookie" to make around the holidays. Which cocoa powder you use makes a big difference. Make sure you choose a high-quality and sustainably sourced cocoa powder, if possible, for best results.

¾ cup high-quality unsweetened cocoa powder, divided
½ cup powdered milk
1 teaspoon instant coffee
½ cup confectioners' sugar
4 tablespoons unsalted butter, at room temperature
¼ cup coffee liqueur

In a bowl, combine ½ cup of the cocoa powder, powdered milk, instant coffee, and confectioners' sugar. Mix well.

In a separate bowl, using an electric mixer, whip the butter until creamy. Slowly add the cocoa mixture until combined. Once the consistency starts to thicken into a paste, add the coffee liqueur and continue to mix.

Scoop about 1 tablespoon of the mixture. Using your hands, form it into a ¾-inch ball. Repeat with the remaining mixture. Place the truffles on a baking sheet and chill in the fridge for 15 minutes.

To finish, roll the truffles in the remaining ¼ cup of unsweetened cocoa powder.

Capirotada

Mexican Bread Pudding / SERVES 6 TO 8

Capirotada is much more than simply bread pudding. That definition is too simplistic and strips away the meaning and history that the dish really holds. Capirotada is something my mama made, just like my Titita before her, and every woman in my family line. After moving to the United States, I went years before hearing or seeing the word capirotada, until one day, while visiting a Mexican store at the end of winter, I saw a sign that said "se vende capirotada." I almost jumped when I saw it. The word alone brought me back to Mexico—it's a dessert that reminds every Mexican of home.

A lot of dishes in Mexico have religious symbolism or relation to a holiday. Capirotada is one of them. The dish made it to the New World along with conquistadores who spread the Catholic religion across Indigenous cultures in Mexico. In post-conquest Mexico, what was originally a savory dish became sweeter as the Aztecs and other Indigenous people used anise tea to soak stale bread and dry meats coming from the Spanish ships. With time, New World ingredients and Indigenous traditions began to create a new version of capirotada, and today each household has their own recipe. Every year, for Catholic Mexicans, Ash Wednesday marks the beginning of the forty-day Lent season that precedes Easter. On Ash Wednesday, and all Fridays during Lent, people fast and abstain from eating meat. Legend has it that capirotada was created to use stale bread before Lent began. Despite the dish being created to be consumed before Lent, it is now one of the most commonly eaten desserts *during* Lent.

Making capirotada is like making lasagna. You work in layers: bread first, then liquid, then nuts, then more bread, on and on until you top the whole thing with melty cheese and sprinkles. Why sprinkles? you may be wondering. And the answer is just because they are fun! At least, that is what my mama would say. Everyone has their own way of making capirotada: some people add more fruit, others cook it on the stove instead of baking it. And now you have the chance to make it your own as well.

4 bolillo rolls (or French rolls)
½ cup (1 stick) unsalted butter, melted
1 ½ cups piloncillo (raw whole cane sugar), or packed dark brown sugar
2 tablespoons fresh orange juice
4 cinnamon sticks
6 whole cloves

3 cups shredded queso Oaxaca
1 cup raisins
1 tablespoon orange zest
½ cup chopped pecans
¼ cup sliced almonds
Rainbow sprinkles, for garnish

Preheat the oven to 350°F and grease a 9-inch round baking dish with butter.

Slice the bread lengthwise into ½-inch thick slices.

Place the melted butter in a shallow bowl. Dip both sides of the bread in the butter, then arrange in a single layer on a sheet pan. Bake for 10 to 15 minutes, flipping halfway through, or until slightly golden.

Meanwhile, in a large saucepan, combine the piloncillo, orange juice, cinnamon sticks, cloves, and 2½ cups of water. Bring to a boil and continue boiling 5 minutes. Reduce the heat to medium-low and simmer, uncovered, until it has a thin syrup consistency, about 20 minutes. Remove from the heat and let the syrup steep for 2 hours (or overnight). Using a strainer, strain the syrup and discard the cinnamon sticks and cloves.

Layer the bottom of the baking dish with a layer of the bread. Using a ladle, slowly spoon some syrup over the bread. Make sure the bread has time to absorb the syrup, so it doesn't pool on the bottom. Otherwise, the pudding will be dry on top. Add a layer of cheese, raisins, orange zest, pecans, and almonds. Continue to layer the bread, syrup, and toppings. Top the last layer of bread with the remaining syrup, raisins, orange zest, nuts, and cheese. Cover the baking dish with aluminum foil and bake for 30 minutes. Remove the foil and bake for another 5 to 10 minutes, or until the cheese is melted, the top crust is golden, and the lower layers are moist.

Serve warm or cold topped with rainbow sprinkles.

Cuernitos

Little Horns / MAKES ABOUT 24 COOKIES

My Titita Tere is not the only woman in my family to have owned a bakery. Tia Maru, my dad's oldest sister, had a bakery adjacent to her home and my grandparents' home. Every Sunday after dinner at my grandparents', she would allow us to go into the bakery and choose a cookie. I always went for cuernitos. My favorite way of eating them was the opposite of how you might imagine eating them. I started with the middle part—the arch—and left the two chocolate-dipped corners for the end. The best parts. Since moving to the United States my Tita Maru has closed her bakery to focus on being a grandmother. Her reputation still follows her—she bakes galletitas and granola out of her kitchen—and she takes pedidos (orders) from her fellow ladies in the neighborhood. The taste of the cookie is very similar to Mexican wedding cookies, which a lot of Americans are familiar with. That taste comes from the pecan meal. The nutty flavor paired with rich chocolate and a cup of hot coffee is pretty much all you will need to make your day better.

1 cup (2 sticks) unsalted butter, at room temperature
½ cup granulated sugar
2 teaspoons pure vanilla extract
2 cups all-purpose flour
1½ cups pecan meal
½ teaspoon sea salt
Confectioners' sugar, for dusting
1 cup semisweet or dark chocolate chips

Preheat the oven to 350°F, and line a baking sheet with parchment paper.

In the bowl of a stand mixer fitted with the paddle attachment, cream the butter, sugar, and vanilla until light and fluffy.

In a medium bowl, combine the flour, pecan meal, and salt. Gradually add to the butter mixture. Mix until a dough ball forms.

Scoop 1 tablespoon of the dough and roll into a log. Place the log on the baking sheet and shape into a crescent moon. Repeat with the remaining dough. Bake the cuernitos for 10 to 12 minutes, or until lightly golden around the edges.

Using a sieve, dust the confectioners' sugar over the warm cookies and let cool completely.

Fill a medium saucepan with a few inches of water and bring to a boil over medium-high heat. Meanwhile, set a heat-proof bowl on top and make sure it doesn't touch the water. Once the water is boiling, reduce the heat to medium.

Add the chocolate to the bowl set over the pot. Using a rubber spatula, stir the chocolate, so it melts evenly and does not burn. Remove from the heat once the chocolate has melted.

Dip both ends of each cuernito in the melted chocolate. Set the cookies on a baking rack allowing the chocolate to cool and harden before serving.

Conchas

Sweet Bread / MAKES 12 CONCHAS

Pan dulce, which literally translates to sweet bread, is used to describe a variety of Mexican pastries. Conchas are part of the pan dulce family. They received their name for the design of their sugar topping, which looks like a sea conch. Pan dulce is an essential part of Mexican breakfast, but it is also eaten at night as a snack during merienda. When I visited Mexico this year, I remembered for the first time in years how robust Mexican breakfast is. We don't really like the idea of brunch in Mexico, because breakfast can extend until eleven o'clock. You start with fruit, then follow with a savory tortilla or egg dish, and just when you think you're full, here comes a pan dulce. Conchas were some of my favorites growing up, and you can find them in all sorts of colors, but the traditional ones are vanilla, chocolate, or strawberry. When eating a concha I like to make a steamy cup of chocolate abuelita (Mexican hot chocolate), slice the concha in half, and dip one end in the foamy milk before taking a bite.

FOR THE DOUGH

1 (14-ounce) packet active dry yeast
½ cup evaporated milk, warmed
⅓ cup granulated sugar
5 tablespoons plus 1 teaspoon unsalted butter, melted
1 large egg
1 teaspoon sea salt
4 cups all-purpose flour
½ teaspoon ground cinnamon
1 teaspoon pure vanilla extract

FOR THE TOPPING

1½ cups (3 sticks) unsalted butter, at room temperature, plus 1 to 2 tablespoons at room temperature for brushing the top of each ball
¾ cup plus 1 tablespoon confectioners' sugar
1 teaspoon pure vanilla extract
1 cup all-purpose flour
2½ teaspoons cocoa powder (optional)

RECIPE CONTINUES ⟶

Make the Dough

Preheat the oven to 375°F, line 2 baking sheets with parchment paper, and grease a large bowl with butter.

In a clean large bowl, combine the yeast with ½ cup warm water and stir. Let the yeast proof for 10 minutes. Add the evaporated milk, granulated sugar, melted butter, egg, and salt. Mix well using a wooden spoon. Gradually add 2 cups of the flour and mix. Add the cinnamon and vanilla extract. Gradually add the remaining 2 cups of flour and mix to form a soft dough that is a bit sticky.

Place the dough on a lightly floured surface. Knead until the dough is smooth and elastic, 3 to 5 minutes. Shape into a ball and transfer the dough to the greased bowl. Rotate the dough in the bowl until evenly coated. Cover with plastic wrap and let rise in a warm place until doubled in size, 60 to 75 minutes.

Conchas / Sweet Bread

Make the Topping

Put the 3 sticks of butter in a medium bowl. Using an electric mixer, cream the butter on medium speed for 30 seconds, or until light and fluffy. Add the confectioners' sugar and continue to beat. Add the vanilla extract. Gradually add the flour and mix until you have a smooth paste.

To make half of the conchas with a chocolate topping, divide the topping into two bowls. Add the cocoa powder to one half and mix well. Set the toppings aside.

Once the bread dough has doubled in size, place on a floured surface. Let it rest for 5 to 10 minutes. Divide the dough into 12 small balls. With lightly floured hands, shape the dough by placing a dough ball on your work surface and rotating the dough as you gently press down.

Arrange the dough balls 3 inches apart on the prepared baking sheets. Using your hands, grease the top of each ball with a little softened butter to help the topping stick to the roll.

Divide the topping into 12 balls. Flatten each ball into a round that is ¼-inch thick. Cover each dough ball with 1 round of topping. Pat down firmly.

Using a sharp paring knife or concha cutter, cut grooves in the topping to give the conchas their traditional design. Cover with plastic wrap and let rise in a warm place until the conchas double in size. This step can take anywhere from 45 to 90 minutes, depending on the temperature of your home. Do not let the conchas rise for more than 2 hours; if they are too big, they won't hold their shape in the oven.

Bake the conchas for 18 to 20 minutes or until they begin to turn golden. Remove from baking sheets and cool on wire racks.

Enjoy warm or cold.

Melón al Vino Blanco con Jengibre

Melon with White Wine and Ginger / SERVES 4 TO 6

In a lot of cultures, fruit is considered dessert. Mexico is no exception. Melón has been one of my favorite fruits since I was little. I loved it in the mornings served with cottage cheese, or in this simple dessert my mom would make in the beginning of summer. I like using piloncillo for this recipe, a minimally processed sugar popular in Mexican and Latin American cuisine; however, fine granulated sugar will do. When making this recipe, you want to make sure the sugar is fully dissolved in the wine sauce. Reserve the mint leaves for the end, so they don't get soggy.

1 medium cantaloupe, halved
and seeds removed
1 cup dry white wine
¾ cup granulated brown sugar
or piloncillo
2 teaspoons minced ginger
6 sprigs mint leaves

Using a melon baller or small ice cream scoop, scoop the cantaloupe into little balls, or cube the melon. Divide into 4 to 6 portions.

In a small bowl, combine the wine, sugar, and ginger. Mix until the sugar has completely dissolved.

Serve the melon in cups and top with the wine sauce and mint.

Peras con Canela en Crema Pastelera

Poached Cinnamon Pears with Mexican Pastry Cream / SERVES 5 TO 6

In ancient Mexico, and more specifically in Aztec civilization, corn was an essential part of life. Native Mexican cultures like the Aztecs believed that humans came from corn, and they would worship the corn god Centeotl and the goddess Chicomecōātl, who was considered the princess of unripe maize. At the beginning of each year, young Aztec men would plant young maize and perform a ritual dance to thank Mother Earth and Centeotl. These dances became increasingly more beautiful and prominent as the warmth of spring and summer brought about great prosperity to the Aztecs in the form of growing maize. Once the corn was ready for harvest, Aztec women would let down their hair and dance among the maize fields to thank Centeotl for his work and for the harvest. Each of the women would pick up five ears of corn and carry them in her arms in a grand procession while singing and dancing. The elder women would also pick up five ears of corn, which they would carefully swaddle and carry on their backs, much like newborn children, all the way to their homes. There they would place the ripe maize into woven baskets outside their doors, where they would stay for over a year until the next season came to represent the resting of the maize gods until the next harvest.

I share this story with you because as you explore Mexican cuisine, you can see and taste that many Mexican dishes are centered around corn. The corn in this recipe comes in the form of cornstarch, specifically the popular drink mix Maizena. You can find this in Mexican grocery stores or it can be found easily online.

This crema pastelera comes from my own grandmother Titita Tere. Her recipe is special in that it does not use eggs, and even more so, that she used this exact crema pastelera recipe for the pastries that she once sold at La Española. This bakery, which she opened the same year my mother was born, enabled her to put all six of her children through college when my grandfather died at the young age of fifty. The silky texture of the cream paired with the tenderness of the pears makes a delicate dessert everyone will enjoy. Be sure to choose pears that are crisp and slightly hard—if you choose a pear that is too ripe this recipe won't turn out well.

FOR THE CREMA PASTELERA
2½ cups whole milk
1 cinnamon stick
1 teaspoon pure vanilla extract
½ (9.9-ounce) can sweetened condensed milk
1 (1.6-ounce) package Maizena vanilla cornstarch drink mix

FOR THE PEARS
5 to 6 red Anjou pears, slightly crisp and underripe
½ cup brown sugar
2 cinnamon sticks

RECIPE CONTINUES →

Peras con Canela en Crema Pastelera / Poached Cinnamon Pears with Mexican Pastry Cream

Make the Crema Pastelera

In a large saucepan, bring the milk to a boil over medium-high heat, while constantly stirring with a wooden spoon so the milk on the bottom of the pan does not burn. Lower the heat to medium heat, and add the cinnamon stick and vanilla. When the cinnamon becomes fragrant, remove it from the milk and add the condensed milk. Continue to cook and mix over medium-high heat for about 2 minutes.

Dissolve the Maizena in ½ cup of room temperature water. Once the milk in the saucepan begins to foam, lower the heat to medium and add the dissolved Maizena. Using a whisk, incorporate the Maizena until fully blended with the milk. Continue gently whisking until it has the consistency of pudding. Once you reach this consistency, remove the cream from the heat. Continue mixing the cream for about 1 minute, then scrape the cream into a medium bowl and cover with parchment paper. You want the parchment paper to touch the top layer of the cream to protect it. Let the cream cool down to room temperature before serving.

Make the Pears

Preheat oven to 350°F and grease the bottom of a deep baking dish with butter.

Do your best to place the pears upright in the dish by leaning them against each other. If they fall over during the baking process that is OK.

In a small bowl, dissolve the brown sugar in 1 cup of water, then pour into the dish with the pears, followed by 4 additional cups of water. Add the cinnamon sticks. Bake for 2½ hours, basting the pears with the sugar-water every 20 minutes. Transfer the pears to a serving dish to cool. Make a syrup to go on top of the pears by using leftover sugar-water: remove and discard the cinnamon sticks and reduce in a saucepan over medium heat until syrupy. (You may also add a shot of rum to make these pears boozy.)

To serve, create a bed of chilled crema pastelera in each serving dish and add the pears on top. Pour the syrup over the pears and serve.

TIP: The cream can be made up to a week in advance and refrigerated. When ready to use the cream, heat it up in the microwave for up to 2 minutes max, and use a whisk to vigorously mix until it has a pudding-like consistency again.

Pan de Muerto

Day of the Dead Bread / SERVES 4 TO 6

Día de Muertos was a significant holiday in my upbringing. My mama would create an altar for our loved ones who had passed and placed an ofrenda for each of them. The altar, which was placed in our windowsill and faced the street, was decorated with bright yellow and orange cempasuchil (marigold) flowers—said to be the flowers of the dead with a fragrance that attracts souls to the altar; alfeñique (sugar) skulls that represent how death can be sweet and not bitter; candles to light the way; and something for the dead to eat. Hence, pan de muerto. In addition, we would add anything our loved ones might miss from the earthly world such as tequila, their favorite music CDs, different candies they enjoyed, their favorite toys, etc. Although the theme during Día de Muertos is, well, death, the tone around the holiday is overall joyous and colorful. Pan de Muerto is an essential part of this celebration. In Mexico, we have a saying surrounding this celebratory bread: En vida o en muerte, no hay persona ni alma que resista comerte. Which translates to "In life or death, there is no person or soul who can resist eating you." There are countless explanations for what the shape of the bread means. But my family's version is that the bread represents the heart and the pieces that form a cross, as well as the nub, represent the skull and bones of the dead. It is said that when our loved ones' souls come to visit, they are nourished by the essence of the bread.

1½ cups bread flour

¼ cup granulated sugar,
    plus 1 cup for coating

Zest of 1 medium lime

Zest of 1 medium orange

½ teaspoon salt

1 (.25 ounce) packet
    instant yeast

½ cup whole milk, room
    temperature

2 large eggs, room
    temperature

4 tablespoons unsalted
    butter, at room
    temperature

¼ cup unsalted butter, melted

Mexican hot chocolate
    for serving

In a stand mixer fitted with the dough hook, combine the flour, sugar, citrus zests, and salt. Mix until well incorporated.

Add the yeast to the room temperature milk, mixing until fully dissolved, then let the mixture rest for 10 minutes.

Add the eggs and butter to the flour mixture and mix until incorporated, then slowly add the milk and yeast mixture. On medium speed, let the mixer incorporate the ingredients until a dough begins to form, separate from the bowl of the mixer, and climb up the hook, approximately 30 minutes. Your dough should be tacky, but not too liquid or sticky.

Grease a medium glass bowl with enough oil to keep the dough from sticking, about 1 tablespoon. Once the dough is ready, add to the bowl, cover loosely with plastic wrap and a kitchen cloth. Let rest in a warm place to rise for 1½ to 2 hours, or until

RECIPE CONTINUES $\longrightarrow$

Pan de Muerto / Day of the Dead Bread

it has doubled in size. I suggest turning on your oven for a little while then turning it off and letting the dough rest near the vent while it rises.

Line a large baking sheet with parchment paper, then lightly flour a clean, dry surface.

Once your dough is ready, using a dough cutter, cut a piece the size of about an orange and set aside. Divide the rest of the dough into 4 equal parts and shape them into small rounds by cupping your hands around them, rolling and dragging them gently towards you, and then tucking them under to make a round shape. Place each round on the baking sheet about 3 inches apart from each other.

Divide the leftover dough into 9 equal pieces. Divide 1 piece into 4 equal parts and using your palms, roll each piece into a small ball. Take the remaining 8 pieces and roll them into ropes about 4 inches in length or long enough to cross over your rounds. These will be your "bones." Spreading your index, middle, and ring finger, gently press down while rolling each rope to resemble bumpy bones.

Wet your fingers with a little bit of water, and trace a cross on each roll, then grab your "bones" and gently make crosses on each round. With more water, wet your fingers and gently press at the intersection of each cross to make a small dimple, then press one of your small balls into the middle of the cross. Repeat with each round until you are out of bones. Cover the loaves gently with plastic wrap and place in a warm place to rise for about 1 hour, or until doubled in size.

Preheat the oven to 325°F and position a rack in the center.

Remove the plastic wrap from the loaves and bake for 20 to 25 minutes, or until golden brown.

Place the 1 cup granulated sugar in a medium bowl.

Let the loaves cool for about 30 minutes, then using a pastry brush, paint the melted butter on each loaf before dipping it in the sugar and sprinkling it with more sugar by hand, so it is evenly coated.

Serve with Mexican hot chocolate. These loaves can be enjoyed warm or cold.

Rosca de Naranja

Orange Bundt Cake / SERVES 6 TO 10

My Titita started baking pies and selling them out of her kitchen window to help support her family. One day, the son of the owner of one of the most famous bakeries in Mexico—Panaderia el Globo—stopped by my Titita's window asking for a place to stay. He had gotten kicked out of his home, and in return for a roof over his head, he suggested to my Titita that he would teach her everything he knew about commercial baking. My Titita accepted, and that is how she started to grow her business, from pies, to coffee cakes, to eventually a full-blown bakery, La Española. After a year, the boy's family took him back, and my Titita continued with her business. One of her most popular cakes was this rosca de naranja. She would only make a certain amount each day, and by closing time it was sold out. It was her most popular cake, and I was lucky enough to get the recipe for it before her Alzheimer's started to worsen. This cake is my Titita's legacy: it's all the years of love and labor that she poured into her children and grandchildren. Her story is what inspired me to write this cookbook, and I knew that it would not be complete without being able to share this part of her with you.

FOR THE CAKE

2½ cups all-purpose flour
2 teaspoons baking powder
¼ teaspoon baking soda
¼ teaspoon sea salt
2 oranges, ends trimmed
1 cup (2 sticks) unsalted
    butter, at room
    temperature
1¼ cups granulated sugar
3 large eggs

FOR THE GLAZE

1½ cups confectioners' sugar,
    plus more as needed
3 tablespoons fresh orange
    juice, plus more as needed
¼ teaspoon pure vanilla
    extract

Make the Cake

Preheat the oven to 325°F and position a rack in the center. Grease a 10-cup Bundt pan with butter. Lightly dust the pan with flour and tap out the excess or use baking spray.

In a medium bowl, whisk together the flour, baking powder, baking soda, and salt and set aside.

Using a paring knife, peel the oranges and remove the pith to keep the cake from tasting bitter. Roughly chop the oranges and remove any seeds. In a food processor or high-speed blender, pulse the oranges until smooth with a bit of texture but not puréed.

In a large bowl, using an electric mixer, beat the butter until creamy, about 1 minute. Gradually add the granulated sugar and beat until light and fluffy, 3 to 4 minutes. One by one, add the eggs and mix well. Add the blended oranges. Briefly mix until combined.

RECIPE CONTINUES ⟶

Rosca de Naranja / Orange Bundt Cake

Slowly add the dry ingredients and mix at a low speed. Be careful not to overmix the batter. Transfer to the prepared pan and smooth out the top with a rubber spatula. Bake until the cake is golden and firm to the touch, 45 to 50 minutes. It's ready when a toothpick stuck in the middle comes out clean. Cool on a baking rack set over a sheet pan for 10 minutes. Release the cake onto the rack and let cool completely.

Make the Glaze
Whisk together the confectioners' sugar, orange juice, and vanilla extract in a small bowl. Adjust taste to preference. If you'd like a thicker glaze, add more confectioners' sugar. For a thinner glaze, add more orange juice.

Pour the glaze over the top of the cooled cake, so it drizzles down the sides. Let the glaze set before serving.

Slice and serve. Store leftover cake at room temperature in an airtight container or a covered cake stand.

RESOURCES

ACKNOWLEDGMENTS

This cookbook would not be here without the unwavering support of extraordinary family and friends who believed in me.

First, I want to thank my parents, Francisco Pons and Lorena Lopez. Thank you for dreaming for your children, taking uncomfortable risks, and protecting Team Pons. You have always reminded Vanessa and me how capable we are, encouraged us to push ourselves, and cheered us on from start to finish. Thank you for taking that leap.

A special thank you to the team at PA Press, including Holly La Due for her incredible partnership and guidance, Lynn Grady, Sara Stemen, and Paul Wagner. And a big, big thank you to Hetty McKinnon, for writing a beautiful foreword I am so proud to have as a part of this book.

I want to thank my friends: Carina Skrobecki, Talia Green, Marissa Alves, Brian Oh, Aj Ragasa, Mackenzie Peters, May Xiong, Delaney Brown, and Kristina Capulong for all of the hours you sacrificed out of your busy lives. Thank you for creating the recipes from my book and photographing the dishes with so much love that I am reminded of my childhood.

Kristina Capulong, I want to give you a special thanks for gifting your beautiful studio Kasama Space so we could photograph additional recipes. Again, thank you for helping me bring my dream to life.

Thank you, Brian Oh, for being the most patient, kind, and supportive human, even as I was going through immigration amidst the pandemic. I cannot thank you enough for being there with me through those darker moments. Thank you for believing in me, encouraging me to pursue this book, and listening to all of my other wild ideas and projects.

Thank you, Matt Ogle, for designing this beautiful book with me. I have no words to describe my appreciation for the countless hours you gave me, experimenting with ideas and advising the design style, layout, and cover. It is above and beyond what I imagined. It is perfect.

Thank you, Erin Motley, for always challenging me with constructive feedback, helping me develop the written pieces, and proofreading every revision. This book would not be possible without your extensive knowledge. There is no one else I would trust to write this story with me.

I want to thank my community for supporting this book and my family. You are contributing toward keeping a family together and allowing my parents to see their native land again. For you, I have nothing but gratitude.

And lastly, I want to thank the women in my family, especially my grandmothers and mom. You have taught me how to confront every obstacle with grace, love, and resilience. I will continue to work hard and love what I love, hoping to become as strong as all of you. Thank you. Las quiero.

INDEX